CRIME SCENES

Revealing the science behind the evidence

Paul Roland

ARCTURUS

CONTENTS

Introduction 6

Chapter 1
WRITTEN IN BLOOD 11
A Brief History of Forensic Science 12
The Death of Lady Mazel 13
Deadly Poisons 14
An Emergent Science 16
The First Detectives 18
New Developments 22
Case File: The Real Sherlock Holmes 23
Case File: Murder Under the Microscope 26

Chapter 2
SCENE OF THE CRIME 29
Securing the Scene 30
Collecting Evidence 35
Forensic Profile: Crime Scene Investigator . . . 39
Preserving Evidence: Forensic Photography . . . 40
The Philosophy of Forensics 42
Forensic Profile: The Coroner 44
Case File: If The Glove Fits –
       The O. J. Simpson File 46

Chapter 3
MATERIAL WITNESSES 51
Bloodstains 52
Footprints and Tyre Tracks 54
The Great Train Robbery 56
Evaluating Prints 58
Incriminating Toolmarks 59
Case File: The Stratton Brothers 60
Case File: The Widow Accused 63
Case File: The On-The-Ball Billionaire 66
Case File: Geographical Forensics –
Driven to Murder 70
Case File: A Case Without A Corpse –
       The Woodchip Killer 72
Case File: The Battered Widow 76

ARCTURUS

Arcturus Publishing Limited
26/27 Bickels Yard
151–153 Bermondsey Street
London SE1 3HA

Published in association with
foulsham
W. Foulsham & Co. Ltd,
The Publishing House, Bennetts Close,
Cippenham, Slough, Berkshire
SL1 5AP, England

ISBN: 978-0-572-03333-0

This edition printed in 2007
Copyright © 2006
Arcturus Publishing Limited

British Library Cataloguing-in-Publication
Data: a catalogue record for this book is
available from the British Library

Printed in China

Jacket and book design: Beatriz Waller
Project editor: Nicky Hodge
Layout: Balley Design Associates

CRIME SCENES

Chapter 4
CRIME LAB 77
Tour of the Crime Lab 78
DNA 79
What is DNA Fingerprinting? 80
Trace Evidence – Under the Microscope 83
Fibres 84
Glass 86
Toxicology 87
Poison 87
The Audio-Visual Lab 90
Case File: A Scraping of Paint 92
Case File: A Murdered Teenager 94
Case File: A Hair Out of Place 97
Case File: Doctor Double Cross 100
Case File: Nicotine Poisoning 102
Case File: The Ghost Writer Caught
                on Tape 104
Case File: DNA Catches a Rapist and
                Murderer 108
Case File: Watergate 110
Case File: A Sharp-Eyed Investigator 111

Chapter 5
ANATOMY OF A MURDER 113
Determining Cause of Death 114
Betrayed by Bugs 117
The Autopsy 118
Tattoos 122
In Suspicious Circumstances –
                Clues to Misadventure 123
Fire and Flame 123
Drowning 123
Case File: The Exact Time of Death 124
Case File: The Mysterious Death of Robert
                Maxwell 127

Chapter 6
FORENSIC ANTHROPOLOGY 135
It's All in the Bones 136
Skull Sculpture 138
The Art of Facial Reconstruction 140
Forensic Profile: Forensic Artist 140
Forensic Profile: Criminal Profiler 142
Case File: The Iron Age Murder Mystery 143
Case File: The Mystery of the Romanovs........146
Case File: The MacIvor Case........................149
Case File: Digital Identikit...........................152
Case File: Odontology – Once Bitten 154
Case File: Last Will and Testament................157
Case File: The Railway Rapist 160

Chapter 7
DEADLY FORCE 163
Ballistics 164
Bomb Scene Investigations 166
Arson 168
Case File: A Fatal Falling Out........................170
Case File: The Libyan Embassy Shooting........172
Case File: Hit and Run 175
Case File: JFK and the Magic Bullet 178
Case File: Mail Order Murder 182
Case File: Lockerbie 185
Case File: The King's Cross Fire 186

Chapter 8
SUSPECT SCIENCE 189
Civil Cases 190
Miscarriages of Justice 191
Untrustworthy Scientists 194
Case File: The Hitler Diaries.........................196
Case File: The Mummy in the Cupboard........198
Case File: The Angel of Death......................200
Case File: Jack the Ripper............................202
Case File: The Finger of Suspicion 205
Index 208

The author gratefully acknowledges
the use of interview material from
The New Detectives and *The FBI
Files* from The Discovery Channel as the
basis for the 'Forensic Profiles' featured
in this book. Thanks also to Court TV's
Crime Library (www.crimelibrary.com
<http://www.crimelibrary.com/>),
Forensic Solutions LLC and CNN's
The Real CSI.

**Illustrations reproduced with the
kind permission of the following:**

AKG Page: *27*

Corbis Pages: *12, 35, 57, 64, 67,
69, 79, 80, 95, 97, 98, 99, 112,
113, 115, 129, 134, 141, 153,
166, 183, 199, 205*

Empics Pages: *65, 101, 159,
171, 184*

Getty Pages: *6, 10, 11, 14, 15, 16,
17, 19, 20, 29, 32, 34, 36, 38, 41,
43, 47, 49, 50, 53, 55, 58, 71, 73,
74, 75, 81, 83, 89, 91, 105, 107,*
*120, 121, 122, 137, 142, 156,
162, 179, 201*

Helga Luest: Page: *155*

**Institut de Police Scientifique,
Switzerland** Pages: *23, 24, 25*

Kobal Collection Pages: *21*

Rex Features
Pages: *117, 130, 145, 147, 148,
161, 163, 165, 167, 168, 173,
174, 181, 185, 187, 188, 189,*
190, 191, 192, 197, 203

Sara Foster Page: *139*

SPL Pages: *85, 78, 93, 103, 109*

The Pantagraph: Pages: *125, 126*

University of Tennessee:
Page: *116*

**West Australian Newspapers
Limited:** Page: *177*

Introduction

The partially clothed body of an unidentified woman is discovered on the front lawn of a house in a quiet, respectable suburban neighbourhood of Florida on a Sunday morning by a man walking his dog. The police are called to the scene, which they secure with yellow perimeter tape printed with the warning 'Crime Scene – Do Not Cross'. An officer ushers the swelling crowd of curious onlookers to the other side of the street, his partner radioing in for a homicide detective and a team of forensic investigators to comb the area for evidence.

The scene will be familiar to regular viewers of the popular US TV series *CSI – Crime Scene Investigation*, which pulls in an audience of more than 50 million in the US and millions more around the world. But this particular crime was real, one of many thousands of homicides reported every day of the year in towns and cities across the globe. The language and the uniforms may differ depending on the country but, sadly, murder is universal and a feature of life that goes all the way back to the day when Cain killed Abel.

Popular TV series like *CSI Miami* have done much to increase public awareness of forensic crime and the techniques now used to catch criminals

Chalk markings on the road record the location of bullet casings

MODERN FORENSICS

In the past the authorities have had to rely on fingerprints, eye witnesses and occasionally the culprit's compulsion to confess, but in recent years forensic science has made incredible advances with the advent of DNA analysis and trace evidence identification techniques that have given investigators what appear to be infallible tools for identifying the guilty and putting them where they belong – behind bars.

In the fictional TV show a single hair, fibre or flake of paint is sufficient to identify the killer, arsonist, robber, rapist or terrorist and place them at the crime scene. With their gleaming laboratory and state-of-the-art, high-tech diagnostic equipment at their disposal, it is usually only a matter of hours before one of the glamorous CSI techs matches the fatal bullet to the suspect's gun or reveals the full history of the deceased from a single hair, leaving the detective in charge of the case to take the 'perp' into custody as the closing credits roll.

If only it were that easy in real life, all the criminals would be in handcuffs and law-abiding citizens could sleep soundly in their beds. While it is true that 'the evidence never lies' and that a single fibre is often sufficient grounds to secure a search warrant or make an arrest, rarely is one

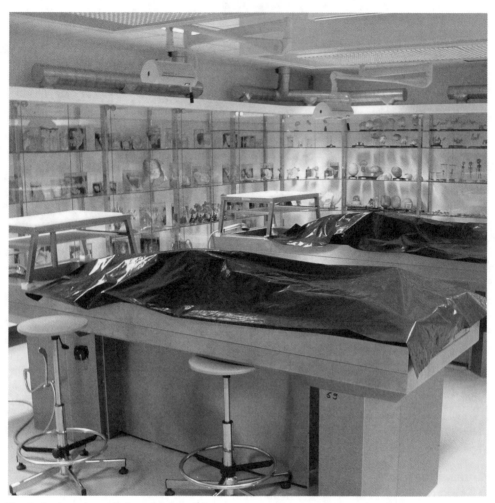

The sterile atmosphere of a forensic science lab

item of evidence enough to send someone to jail or the electric chair. In the real world the law demands irrefutable physical evidence backed up by eye-witness testimony and preferably a confession too, if a conviction is to be secured. However, suspects are rarely as cooperative in real life as they appear to be on TV. They don't give up their liberty without a fight and the police never underestimate the ability of a smart lawyer to undermine witness testimony and discredit evidence in the hope of raising the spectre of 'reasonable doubt'.

Fortunately forensic science is continually developing, making it increasingly difficult for criminals to get away with their crimes. But unlike their elegant, ever-active fictional counterparts, the real CSIs – crime scene investigators – rarely get the chance to confront a suspect unless they are called to testify in court. Many are laboratory technicians who specialize in one area of forensic science. Forensic biologists scrutinize human trace evidence such as blood, hair and saliva. Forensic chemists analyze chemical residue for traces of drugs, explosives, paint and so forth. Forensic anthropologists can evaluate the sex, age and identity of a person from their bones and there are even forensic meteorologists who can supply vital clues regarding the weather at the crime site at a given time or day. When there are no eye witnesses, science can become the silent witness which places a criminal at the scene of the crime. A notable example can be the car which carries traces of mud from the location or is found in the killer's garage covered in rain droplets although it hasn't rained in his neighbourhood for days, but has done so miles away at the scene of the crime.

Unfortunately, although procedural police shows have increased public awareness of forensic techniques they have not dissuaded habitual criminals, and it could be argued that it has actually created an unrealistic expectation in the public mind regarding the speed and infallibility of forensic detection. It must be remembered that CODIS, the criminal database, can only produce a positive match if a criminal's DNA or fingerprints are in the system. A killer without a record remains anonymous and at large. As one forensic expert ruefully admitted, 'We have an imperfect human being using imperfect science striving for a perfect conclusion.' Killers can elude the police for years until they make a fatal error, or are caught in the act by chance because they reoffend. It is only then that all the carpet fibres, fingerprints, flakes of paint and other forensic evidence can be presented in the hope of forcing the perpetrator to confess to their crimes or cut a deal with detectives to give up their accomplices, or offer leads in other cases, if they have any.

THE REALITY OF FORENSICS

Nevertheless, thanks to the popularity of *CSI* and the many true crime shows which have sprung up in its wake, forensic science is now the fashionable career choice. Applications have reached record levels in every country where a college or academy is offering courses. But when they graduate, today's students will discover that real CSIs have a far harder time cracking cases than their TV counterparts. They won't be questioning suspects, nor swarming over a crime scene in Beverley Hills in Nike trainers. They will spend most of their time in the laboratory pouring over reference books, peering down microscopes and conducting mundane, repetitive tests. And although technical advances will enable them to identify the component parts of even the most minute trace evidence, they could wait weeks or even months for a test result if the laboratory is overwhelmed, as is frequently the case.

For example, at the Los Angeles County Coroner's Office, the world's largest forensic facility, a staff of 64 process 8,000–10,000 bodies a year, 24 hours a day, 364 days a year. Under such pressure it is perhaps no surprise that investigators are forced to prioritize their cases and that many freely admit that the sheer scale of the problem and lack of human resources means that many criminals are literally getting away with murder. Frequently forensic science helps to convict a guilty person only after they have made the one crucial mistake which has brought them to the attention of the police. Law enforcement now has extraordinarily sophisticated tools to help solve the puzzle posed by the crime scene, but even those at the cutting edge of the new technology admit that there are times when science is no substitute for old-fashioned, dogged detective work.

EXAMINING A CRIMINAL INVESTIGATION

In the following pages we go behind the scenes of a criminal investigation, putting the once secret science of forensic detection under the microscope. You will discover how evidence is collected and analyzed, what clues can be obtained from a crime scene and a corpse, what happens at an autopsy and how computer technology is being used in the worldwide crusade against crime. Specific forensic techniques are

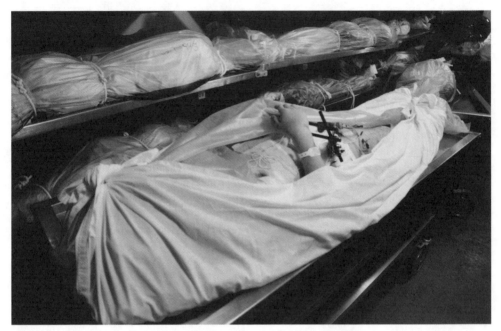

At any one time, the main crypt at LA County Coroner's Office is full to overflowing

described in detail, including how a pathologist accurately determines the time and cause of death and how anonymous victims can be identified from a pile of bones.

We also reveal how a medical examiner can tell whether the body on the mortuary slab has died of natural causes, or as a result of suicide, accident or foul play – and what part blood splatter, ballistics and computer programs play in re-creating the crime scene.

There is inevitably a heavy emphasis on murder cases because they are the most serious crimes a person can commit and they frequently stretch the resources and resourcefulness of investigators. However, every major category of crime is covered including arson, abduction, rape, robbery and terrorism as well as tragic accidents involving loss of life and cases in which forensic science was used to overturn a wrongful conviction and expose a serious miscarriage of justice.

If you want to know exactly how DNA,

toxicology, trace evidence analysis and forensic entomology can break an apparently airtight alibi, you will find it here, where each aspect of the investigation is illustrated by real cases taken from the files of law enforcement agencies around the world, many of them appearing in print for the very first time. And if you actually do have a serious interest in becoming a real CSI yourself, this book should prepare you for what you can expect to deal with in the hard but rewarding world of forensic science.

Be warned that there is no easy route – you will normally need multiple degrees in several sciences as well as a thorough medical knowledge and, needless to say, a strong stomach. But if you can remain detached and dedicated to uncovering the facts you could find yourself contributing to the solution of baffling crimes, while making society far safer by proving the guilt of dangerous criminals and perhaps even bringing closure to bereaved families.

Since ancient times the scientifically minded have searched for reliable ways of determining the cause of suspicious deaths and identifying those responsible for committing serious crimes. In the days before the advent of DNA profiling and all the other high-tech tools of modern forensic science, the detection of crime depended almost entirely on the luck and dogged determination of the investigator. Unfortunately, there were those both within the legal system and without who doubted the reliability of the emerging science or who attempted to block its progress for selfish ends. In modern times such reservations were swept aside as forensic detection proved that it had the power to nail a suspect.

A BRIEF HISTORY OF FORENSIC SCIENCE

It has been said that the patron saint of forensic science is St Thomas the Doubter, who is as loyal a disciple as his brothers but cannot bring himself to accept as a fact anything he has not seen with his own eyes. Of the Resurrection of Jesus he says, 'Except I shall see in his hands the print of the nails, and put my finger into the print of the nails, and thrust my hand into his side, I will not believe.' (John 20:25)

He remains a good model for forensic scientists of all faiths and those of none.

The Bible has more than its share of murders, rapes and random cruelty, but it is safe to assume that the first homicide must have occurred even further back when the first Neanderthal crushed the skull of his neighbour with a rock or animal bone in a dispute over food, water or a mate, proving that human nature has changed little over the millennia. However, in the course of human evolution we became social animals and acquired the need for laws and ways of enforcing the laws.

Justice or a sense of fairness demanded a way of proving innocence or guilt which was initially served by trial by combat and trial by ordeal, but was ultimately determined by an independent judicial system of trial by judge or jury.

Trial by ordeal: forcing the accused to walk on hot metal was standard before proper trials were established

Forensic science, meaning science in service to the law, is a comparatively recent discipline but it has evolved in faltering stages since ancient times. The Roman physician Antistius performed one of the earliest recorded post-mortems to determine which of the 23 stab wounds that felled Julius Caesar was the fatal blow. But the first recorded reference to forensic detection dates from the Middle Ages. A Chinese book called *Hsi Duan Yu* (roughly translated as The Washing Away of Wrongs) described the distinctive marks and wounds which reveal the cause of death, accidental and otherwise.

During the Renaissance, Fortunato Fidelis learned how to distinguish between accidental and deliberate drowning, while his fellow countryman Paolo Zacchia catalogued fatal wounds by blade, bullet and ligature in order to establish a criteria for determining whether a body had met its end by suicide, natural causes or murder. His findings, together with those of the anatomist Morgagni, can be seen as cementing the cornerstones of modern pathology.

THE DEATH OF LADY MAZEL

But although the infant forensic sciences were already evolving, cynicism and bullheadedness continued to plague criminal investigations. Even when there was a profusion of physical evidence, its significance was rarely understood or appreciated. When the early 16th-century Parisian aristocrat Lady Mazel was found stabbed to death in her bed with an embarrassment of clues to choose from, the authorities displayed an alarming lack of imagination that led to the false imprisonment and death of an innocent man.

The servants had been forced to break down her Ladyship's bedroom door after she had failed to respond to their entreaties. Her strongbox had been rifled and a gold watch was also missing, but the curious aspect was that her door possessed a spring lock which automatically locked from the inside so no one could enter during the night.

A clasp knife was recovered from the fireplace and a cheap lace cravat and a discarded napkin were found among the rumpled bedclothes. The latter had been folded to form a makeshift nightcap. Assuming it to belong to her Ladyship's attacker, it was passed among the servants until it was found to fit her valet, a man named Le Brun. It later transpired that the cravat had belonged to a footman named Berry who had been summarily dismissed, but this fact was ignored as irrelevant. As Le Brun did not have any incriminating blood spots on his clothes it was assumed that he had let an accomplice in through the kitchen door and then into her Ladyship's bedroom using a skeleton key that he was known to possess. A more exhaustive search of the house led to the discovery of a bloodstained nightshirt in the attic which, inconveniently for the authorities, did not fit their suspect. Nevertheless the hapless Le Brun was tortured and died from his injuries.

THE REAL MURDERER DISCOVERED

The following month Berry, the footman, was arrested in the vicinity on an unrelated matter and found to have Lady Mazel's watch on his person. He freely confessed to her murder and described how he had slipped unnoticed into the house and hidden in the attic where he lived for several days on bread and apples. He had waited until the household had departed for church on Sunday morning before emerging from his hiding place and lying under Lady Mazel's bed until she retired that night. For some reason he had felt the need to make an improvised nightcap from a napkin which had fallen off in the struggle after her Ladyship awoke to find him rifling her strongbox. After stabbing her he hid the bloodstained nightshirt in the attic in case it was found on him as he left the house, but he had evidently forgotten about the nightcap.

Had the authorities made a thorough search of the attic they might have also found discarded apple cores and breadcrumbs which, together with the nightcap and bloodstained nightshirt, would have confirmed the presence of an uninvited

Lady Mazel's footman described how he had hidden in the attic for several days

overnight guest. The valet would have no need of a makeshift nightcap, nor would he have worn a cheap cravat, but the mere mention of the dismissed servant should have aroused suspicion.

Such incidents demonstrate that those who investigate crime and administer justice must be alive to all the facts and the possibilities they present and not simply set out to select those which support their personal theory. The application of forensic science alone cannot ensure that the guilty are always identified and the innocent exonerated.

DEADLY POISONS

At the time of the Renaissance, poisoning was practically an art form. Since ancient times it had

been the preferred method of dispatching both enemies and tiresome lovers by virtue of it being practically undetectable and the fact that it could be administered surreptitiously, without recourse to violence. But even in the age of scholarship and science, techniques for detecting its presence were still woefully inadequate and unreliable.

The inquest into the death of the Earl of Atholl in 1579 is typical of the period. Suspecting poison, an attending physician cut open the corpse and dipped his finger into the contents of the nobleman's stomach. A single taste was sufficient to confirm the presence of poison and make the doctor very sick indeed.

By the early years of the 19th century there was

a profusion of new poisons which could be purchased freely over the counter and which even the most renowned chemists had difficulty in detecting. Many, such as arsenic, strychnine, morphine and nicotine, were used in small doses for medicinal purposes, which made it difficult to determine whether they had been administered innocently or with malicious intent. Moreover, some occurred naturally in the body post-mortem, a little-known fact which had led to the false conviction of many innocent individuals. As late as the 19th century it was a revelation to even the most experienced chemists that arsenic can seep into a coffin from the surrounding soil and be absorbed into the body, a process which led at least one physician to conclude that a body he had exhumed had been unnaturally hastened to the grave by the administration of deadly poison. The deceased man's innocent son was consequently accused of the crime and executed.

Inevitably it became a matter of urgency to develop reliable new techniques for the detection and identification of toxins in the body. Fortunately, necessity again proved to be the mother of invention and in 1813 a precociously gifted Spanish medical graduate known simply as Orfila found himself faced with a unique problem. Having promised his eager audience of fellow students in the Paris School of Medicine that a certain reaction would occur when arsenous acid was mixed with various liquids, he was shocked to discover that it was not so. Further experiments using other liquids also failed to produce the expected results, whereupon the embarrassed

In the early part of the 19th century a profusion of new poisons was freely available at the chemist

lecturer dismissed his class and spent the rest of the day scouring the shelves of the university library in search of the solution.

After hours of fruitless inquiry Orfila had his 'eureka' moment and realized that he couldn't find the answer for the simple reason that the first toxicology textbook hadn't yet been written. So he set himself the task of doing just that and within the year had published his seminal *Treatise On Poisons*, thereby earning himself a place in the history of forensic science and severely curtailing the lucrative trade in poisonous philtres, pills and potions at a stroke.

AN EMERGENT SCIENCE

In our age of routine DNA testing, spectroscopic analysis and global fingerprint databases it is almost impossible to appreciate the degree of suspicion with which the emerging science was seen by both the judiciary and the general population. The Church repeatedly urged Christians of all denominations to spurn the new disciplines which they saw as tantamount to questioning the will of God.

Small doses of poison were routinely used for medicinal purposes

In many countries suspicion alone was enough to subject a suspect to torture in the hope of extracting a confession and there was no way of knowing if it was a genuine declaration of guilt or offered simply to end their suffering. Even judges could be blinded to reason by their unswerving allegiance to the letter of the law, which they saw as chiselled in stone, sacred and absolute. In one of the first studies of crime and criminals (*Mysteries of Police and Crime*, 1898), the author, Major Arthur Griffiths, recounts the true story of a Maltese judge who, in the early years of the 18th century, had knowingly condemned an innocent man to death because the circumstantial evidence against him was compelling. The judge knew the man to be innocent because he himself had witnessed the crime and had seen the murderer with his own eyes, but his blinkered loyalty to legal formalities and inflexibility prevented him from acting as a witness in the case and publishing what he considered to be 'privileged information'. So he had ordered the suspect to be tortured and then executed following the extraction of a forced 'confession'.

Such incidents were comparatively common in the centuries before the adoption of the central precept of European law, which states that a suspect is considered innocent until proven guilty beyond a reasonable doubt.

It wasn't until 1752 that the first true test case for the emergent science made its appearance in a European court of law. At the trial of the poisoner Mary Blandy, expert witness Dr Anthony Addington was asked how he could prove that a packet of white powder found at the defendant's home was arsenic. He replied that it was of the same consistency and texture as arsenic and that it had produced thick white plumes of vapour when placed on a red-hot iron just as arsenic would do. Therefore it followed that the substance which had been found on the defendant was indeed arsenic. This pronouncement qualifies Dr Addington as the first expert witness in a modern trial.

Confessions were extracted by torture at the hands of the Spanish Inquisition (c1500)

SCIENTIFIC DETECTION

The first recorded example of scientific detection occurred in Scotland 34 years later. A young pregnant girl had been found with her throat cut in an isolated cottage on her parent's farm in Kirkcudbright. The local doctor concluded that the killer was evidently left-handed as the cut had been made from right to left and there were further clues in the vicinity which invited investigation. A trail of footprints were found on soft boggy ground nearby, with deep impressions at the toe indicating that whoever had made them had been running from the scene. Drops of blood were also found, as was a bloody handprint on a stile over which the murderer must have climbed in order to escape.

Plaster casts were made of the prints, which gave the police a template for comparison and served to preserve the distinctive features of the boots, which had recently been mended and shod with iron nails. All adult males on surrounding farms were asked to submit to an examination of their boots and shoes, which produced a positive match with those owned by a left-handed labourer named Richardson. But he appeared to have an alibi – he was with two other farmworkers at the time of the crime. However, when questioned, they recalled that he had left them to gather nuts in a wood near the girl's farm and returned half an hour later with a scratch on his face and mud on his stockings. A search of his cottage produced the stockings, which turned out to be both muddy and bloodstained, prompting a comparison to be made with the mud in which the footprints were found. Both contained a trace of sand which was unique to the boggy ground near the victim's farm. Faced with such indisputable physical evidence Richardson had little choice but to confess in an effort to unburden his conscience before his execution.

The fact that the crime occurred in a remote rural region meant that the police could safely assume that the culprit was a local man and so had only to eliminate the innocent from a small number of suspects to identify the guilty party.

THE FIRST DETECTIVES

By the mid-19th century England had its first full-time professional detectives and America had its Pinkerton agents, but modern forensic science was still in its infancy and was neither entirely trusted by the police nor the public, which meant that juries could ignore circumstantial evidence if they disliked the face or manner of the accused. In its place were well-meaning but crude, impractical attempts at criminal classification such as Bertillonage, which, in the days before photography, used a complex system of physical measurements to identify criminals, and the spurious science of phrenology – determining a person's criminal inclinations from the shape of their skull and the measurements of facial features (which led to the evil of eugenics). Both were soon rendered redundant by the much more reliable mapping of fingerprints.

In the 1870s a British civil servant in India, William Herschel, had been entrusted with organizing pension payments to ex-soldiers, but couldn't distinguish native applicants on facial features alone. Anxious that he shouldn't pay the same person twice, he devised a method of infallible identification which required the applicant to sign for their money with a thumbprint in ink – a practice thought to have been originated by the ancient Chinese. Shortly thereafter a Scottish physician, Dr Henry Faulds, saw the potential of fingerprinting in the fight against crime and devised a system for categorizing and classifying prints according to the whorls and ridges which made each person's fingerprint unique.

But until the late 19th century, when fingerprinting was proven to be both reliable and practical, criminal detection was a simple matter of dogged persistence, luck and intuition. Suspects were eliminated only if they could furnish an alibi corroborated by witnesses of good character, while circumstantial evidence was often sufficient to condemn a man to imprisonment or death. The authorities relied on a criminal's compulsion to confess rather than physical evidence.

Homer S. Cummings who showed that evidence alone can be used to reconstruct a crime

Then, in 1924, a youthful state's attorney made American legal history by demonstrating that, in the absence of reliable eye witnesses, evidence alone can be used to reconstruct a crime.

In February of that year Harold Israel, an itinerant, alcoholic First World War veteran, was arrested in Norwalk, Connecticut on suspicion of having murdered a priest in nearby Bridgeport. Father Hubert Dahme had been slain in full view of several witnesses on Main Street by a single bullet from a .32 revolver, the same calibre weapon as was found on the soldier when he was questioned. Under unrelenting interrogation Harold broke down and confessed to killing the priest out of sheer desperation and despair. But the State's Attorney, Homer Cummings, was uneasy. As he looked over the evidence a number of unanswered questions nagged at him until he felt compelled to revisit the scene and question the witnesses himself. Why, he wondered, had Israel held onto the revolver when selling it would have brought the starving soldier a hot meal and a comfortable bed in a warm boarding house instead of the draughty dilapidated room he shared with two other veterans in a freezing flophouse? And why did the soldier shoot Father Dahme in the back if he was as angry as he claimed to be? Surely he would have confronted the priest and poured out his rage face to face?

When Cummings made further enquiries he discovered that the police had found not one but dozens of spent .32 shell casings at the ex-soldier's lodgings. Apparently all three men had been in the habit of shooting their revolvers from the window at empty liquor bottles for target practice. Any of the three could have fired the fatal bullet and, if not, there were millions of mass-produced .32

The father of fingerprinting: William Herschel

revolvers in circulation at that time with no reliable method for determining which weapon had fired a particular round.

As soon as the police had extracted the confession, Israel was allowed his first full night's sleep in days and the next morning retracted it, claiming that it had been forced from him under duress. But his alibi was weak.

He claimed to have been at the movies watching a film called *The Leather Pushers*, but when pressed he couldn't remember the plot. Cummings asked at his own office if anyone had seen the film and those who had shared an equally vague recollection. Low-budget production line 'flicks' in the silent era were not renowned for the strength of their storylines.

Convinced that there was sufficient doubt not to proceed with the prosecution case, Cummings re-enacted the murder on Bridgeport's Main Street with his assistants standing in for the eye witnesses. It was obvious to Cummings that the single street lamp was too far from the spot where the priest had fallen to give the witnesses a clear view of the attacker in the encroaching evening gloom. He would have been no more than a shadow. It would have been impossible even to describe the clothes he had been wearing. No doubt the description published in the newspapers had supplied the details given by witnesses.

DISMISSING THE FINAL WITNESS

The only witness remaining was a waitress at a hamburger diner who claimed that Israel had been a regular customer and that she had waved to him through the window as he passed the diner just before the priest was killed. But when Cummings went inside to question her he noticed that the window was steamed up that time of the evening, obscuring a clear view of the street. Wiping the condensation with his sleeve, the prosecutor found that he still couldn't recognize his own colleagues because of the glare of the street lights on the wet window. Finally, he asked the waitress to wave to him when he passed outside to indicate that she

Boomerang (1947) was inspired by the real-life case that Homer Cummings solved from physical evidence alone

Increased security at airports is now commonplace

specific firearm. But sex crimes remained stubbornly and frustratingly problematic until science took a quantum leap into the digital age with the discovery and practical application of DNA analysis in the 1980s.

The realization that every individual has a unique molecular fingerprint – with the exception of identical twins – meant that scientists need only a scraping of skin or a drop of blood or saliva to identify the donor. Now, no matter how careful or thorough a criminal might be in eradicating evidence, they cannot avoid leaving a tell-tale trace on their victim or at the scene.

Forensic science is the one branch of science that cannot afford to become complacent. New techniques of crime detection need to be and are being developed and eagerly assimilated by crime prevention agencies.

For example, increased anxiety concerning travel security has resulted in the use of particle analysis equipment being installed at many international airports. All luggage is now routinely swabbed and screened for traces of explosive, as are passengers, who now have to pass through a metal screening arch.

Another recent innovation is the use of specialized software which can identify the make and model of the printer which sourced a particular document such as a fake passport, counterfeit currency, ID or ransom note. It can scan the minute bands of light and dark which all printers produce on the suspect item and match them to a specific make and model of printer.

Every new development in the fields of medicine, chemistry and even aeronautics technology is scrutinized and evaluated by leading forensic scientists to see if there is a possibility that it might prove useful.

And thanks to the massive current popularity of forensic science-based TV crime shows there are now more recruits to the ranks of crime prevention and detection agencies than ever before, stacking the odds for the first time ever in favour of a law-abiding society.

had recognized him. Cummings walked past three times but she failed to acknowledge him every time. Instead she waved to two strangers and one of Cummings' assistants.

It transpired the girl had been encouraged to concoct her story by a lawyer friend with whom she was hoping to share the reward. The charges against Harold Israel were subsequently dropped and he seized his second chance at life, becoming a happily married, wealthy businessman while Homer Cummings rose to become America's youngest attorney general.

The case inspired a Hollywood movie, but the most significant aspect was the fact that it thereafter became common knowledge that every crime scene holds clues that are usually more reliable than even the best-intentioned witnesses. Baffling crimes could be reconstructed from the physical evidence alone and the guilty convicted with confidence.

NEW DEVELOPMENTS

During the following decades developments in ballistic science provided investigators with the means of matching a bullet or shell casing to a

case file

The Real Sherlock Holmes

Forensic technology may be a comparatively recent development, but the science, or art, of forensic detection is as old as crime itself. Even without the aid of genetic fingerprinting, trace evidence analysis and crime scene reconstruction software, an astute investigator could apply simple scientific methods to solve even the most baffling cases.

One such man was Professor R. A. Reiss, a French criminologist and founder of the Institute of Police Science in Lausanne. During a visit to Le Havre in 1909 Professor Reiss was invited by the local police to assist in the investigation into the murder of a female 'fence', a dealer in stolen goods. The back of her skull had been crushed by a single blow while she sat at a table nursing an empty bottle of liquor, her back to her assailant. An empty cupboard indicated that the motive must have been robbery, but other than that there were no clues – at least that is what the local prefect of police assured Reiss as he knelt by the victim's front door with his magnifying glass in hand. But the professor was a patient and persistent man with an unerring eye for detail. Within moments he had discovered a single drop of blood and was following the trail on all fours down the passage to the room where the body had been found. Apparently the murderer had been nicked by a splinter when he had jemmied open

Professor R. A. Reiss in Brazil (right, wearing cap) preparing for an excursion in 1913

Reiss's office in 1910

the door and had left a trail of tiny droplets which the gendarmes had overlooked.

But there was more. Rising to his feet, the professor declared that the killer was a left-handed man who was known to the deceased and that he had killed her after she surprised him rifling through her cupboard in the dark. Asked how he could know this without having been an eye witness, Reiss remarked that it was a simple matter of observation and deductive reasoning. The blood spots were on the left side of the passage and a trail of tiny specks of candle grease were on the right, indicating that the murderer held the tool for prising open the door in his left hand and the candle in his right, which is the opposite of what a right-handed person would do. The fatal blow was on the left-hand side of the woman's head, confirming that the weapon had been held in his left hand.

The empty bottle and smell of liquor on her revealed that the dead woman had been drunk, and the intruder must have known that it was her habit to drink heavily after dark as he had jemmied the door open without being afraid that he would wake her at that late hour. He had brought the candle with him, as the wax spots began at the beginning of the passage, and he had known which cupboard to search, for nothing else had been disturbed. There were a number of grease spots on the rug in front of the cupboard, which proved that he had searched in the darkness.

While the prefect scratched his head and pondered the significance of these clues, the professor took a scraping of the candle grease and deposited it in an envelope together with two hairs he had plucked from the carpet with tweezers. They were too short to have come from the head of the victim and could prove significant once Reiss had a chance to study them under a microscope.

SCIENCE PROVIDES THE PROOF

The following day the professor arrived at the prefect's office with a detailed description of the man they were seeking. He was a left-handed sailor who had recently returned from Sicily and could be identified by his red moustache and a cut on his left hand where he had been nicked by the splinter. The short red hairs were evidently from a moustache, a chemical analysis of the candle grease revealed a recipe unique to Sicily and the most likely person to bring a candle from Sicily to the port of Le Havre is a sailor. Inquiries at the port led the police to the only ship to have recently arrived from Sicily, where they found an Italian by the name of Forfarazzo who answered the description Reiss had given them.

The final scene played out like a stage melodrama. Forfarazzo was handcuffed and dragged to the scene of the crime where Reiss presented him with a blank sheet of paper claiming it was a letter in order that the suspect would accept it. Forfarazzo took it in his left hand. A search through his pockets recovered the stump of the candle which was revealed to have the same chemical composition as the candle grease found at the murder scene. Yet still Forfazzo refused to make a full confession until the evening of his execution, when he admitted selling his victim the liquor knowing she would be drunk by the time he returned to relieve her of her cash.

Arthur Conan Doyle could not have found a finer model for his fictional detective than R. A. Reiss (centre)

Murder Under the Microscope

In past centuries the aristocracy considered themselves to be above the law and as such immune to prosecution. It was not unknown for a member of the nobility to exercise their power over their own servants to confirm their version of events under the implicit threat of dismissal, or to exploit their influence with the local magistrate to overlook an 'indiscretion', such as the murder of a mistress or servant who would have been considered a mere chattel. Even as late as the Edwardian era the authorities were obliged to accept the word of a gentleman without question, until the evidence proved otherwise. But this genteel world began to crumble with the solution of the notorious Praslin affair – the first crime to be solved using a microscope.

In the summer of 1847 the marriage of the French Duc de Choiseul-Praslin and his wife Fanny was under severe strain. The Duc had refused to give up his pretty mistress, a former governess to the nine Praslin children, while Fanny, the daughter of one of Bonaparte's generals, was in no mood to compromise. It was clearly fated to come to a tragic end.

MURDER AT NIGHT

In the early hours of 18 August, the servants were roused from their beds by a hideous shriek issuing from the Duchesse's bedroom and the violent ringing of her bell as she attempted to summon help. The door was barred from the inside and as the servants debated what to do they heard a crash followed by a ghastly silence. Rushing out into the garden, they looked up as the window was flung open and the Duc appeared in some distress. Assuming that he had interrupted an intruder the servants raced back upstairs to give their master some assistance, but when they entered the now unlocked room they saw only the bruised and battered body of the Duchesse, her throat cut, lying amid overturned furniture. Into this chaotic scene marched the Duc, feigning surprise at finding his wife apparently murdered by burglars. The servants knew better than to question their master, but

Servants were often exploited by unscrupulous employers who could threaten them with dismissal

fortunately for them two gendarmes happened to be passing the house that moment and questioned the witnesses before the Duc had time to coach them in his version of events.

In due course, M. Allard, the head of the Sûreté, was summoned and immediately dismissed the idea of an intruder. The Duchesse's jewels had not been taken and no one had seen strangers fleeing from the house, which had been roused by the commotion.

A search of the Duchesse's room led to the discovery of a blood-stained pistol which the Duc readily admitted to be his own. He had brought it with him, he said, to tackle the intruder, but when he saw his wife's body he had dropped it and it must have been kicked under a sofa in the ensuing confusion. The Duc could account for the blood on his nightshirt, too. It must have been soiled, he argued, when he cradled his wife in his arms as she lay dying, but he couldn't explain the presence in his room of a blood-stained knife or the severed cord from the bell-pull on which she had tugged to summon help. In his anxiety to hide the knife and the cord he had evidently returned to his room while the servants were running in from the garden and had hidden them in the hope of disposing of them at a later date.

Even with such damning evidence M. Allard knew that he would have a hard time convincing a judge of the Duc's guilt. All of it could be explained as the result of irrational actions by a grief-stricken husband, while the servants could not be relied upon to give evidence against their master. Allard would have to trust the pistol to tell the true story. Had it been dropped in the blood as the Duc had claimed, or had it been used to bludgeon the Duchesse to death? It was immediately handed over to the most eminent pathologist in Paris, Ambroise Tardieu, who examined it under the revealing lens of his microscope. There were strands of chestnut hair and fleshy tissue near the trigger and on the butt which matched those of the Duchesse. It was clear that the Duc had tried to cut his wife's throat, but when she resisted he had struck her repeatedly with the pistol. During a medical examination toothmarks were found on the Duc's leg where his wife had bitten him in a last desperate effort to be free of her attacker. Faced with the humiliation of a public execution, the Duc swallowed a lethal dose of arsenic and died in agony three days later.

Chapter 2
Scene of the Crime

Nowadays there's no doubting the popularity of TV crime shows although they can give the false impression that forensic science is completely infallible. This in turn has brought increasing pressure on investigators who are having to become experts in one particular area of forensic detection to meet the higher expectations of juries who have to weigh the evidence. Investigations are no longer solved by a lone detective working on a hunch, but by a highly specialised team working closely together. But even the most damning evidence can be compromised by shoddy police procedures as high-profile cases such as the Nicole Brown Simpson homicide have revealed.

SECURING THE SCENE

When a crime is committed, the first officers to respond are responsible for securing the scene and preserving it as they found it. This means ensuring that nothing is touched or moved so that any physical evidence is not compromised or contaminated. If there are victims displaying signs of life the police will call a team of paramedics to give on-site assistance, if they are not already there in response to the initial emergency call. The injured can then be removed to hospital, but the dead are left as they were found since vital clues can be obtained from studying the position and

condition of the victim. Rigor mortis, for example, which occurs when the heart stops, depriving the muscles of oxygen, can give a clue as to the time of death, but can be broken if the body is handled, while lividity (the discoloration of the skin after death) could change if the body is moved.

In due course a designated crime scene officer will take control of the site, but until then, during the first vital minutes of an investigation, the officers will make preliminary observations and interview any witnesses who are at the scene. An attempt will be made to keep surviving victims calm and isolated so that they can be interviewed

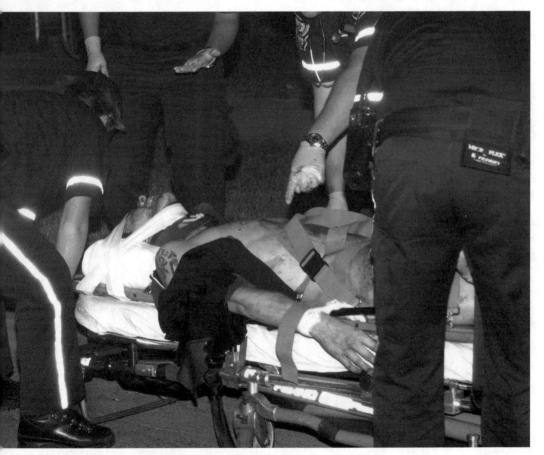

A victim of a shooting is stretchered away by paramedics

A young victim looks on helplessly as her friend receives treatment

while the details and impressions are still fresh in their minds. They will also be discouraged from cleaning themselves up in case they have trace evidence on their clothes, their skin or in their hair.

If the police find the perpetrators they will read them their rights and take them into custody, but it is not their job to investigate, only to identify who was at the location and to record the facts as they found them. Securing the scene also involves ensuring that the area has been thoroughly searched in case a suspect is hiding on, or near, the premises, posing a threat to the paramedics and the investigating unit.

THE NEXT STEP

Once the senior investigating officer is on site, he or she will begin by interviewing the officers who were first on the scene to get their initial impression of the location and the behaviour of those who were directly involved. He or she may find it necessary to request the assistance of more than one team if there are multiple sites; for example, in a murder enquiry the suspect's residence will require searching as well as the site where the body of the victim has been discovered. Each team is led by a crime scene controller who answers to a supervisor. The supervisor then reports to the investigating officer.

Usually the crime scene is a house, an apartment, commercial building or vehicle, all of which can be sealed off and examined in the minutest detail. And if a murder or violent attack has occurred in one area of a building, the whole property will be considered relevant to the case and will be scoured for clues. There may, for example, be evidence in the bathroom where the perpetrator has attempted to clean blood off their hands or tell-tale marks of forced entry at a window or door.

But if it is an exterior location police may have to extend the perimeter to include vehicle tyre tracks, footprints and areas where there is a chance of finding personal items, discarded cigarette butts, a weapon or trace evidence which might have been snagged on undergrowth. If it is a burial site for murder victims there could be other makeshift graves in the area, all of which will have to be excavated, photographed and combed for physical evidence. Exterior scenes may also have to be isolated by a tent to protect evidence from the effects of the weather and to exclude the prying eyes of curiosity-seekers and the media.

The FBI erect a tent to exhume a body in an attempt to gain more evidence

In the case of a terrorist atrocity involving an explosion the scene can extend for several miles and every inch of that area has to be sealed off and searched for the minutest fragments of the device in the hope that it can be pieced together again to give vital clues. In the rare cases where a wounded victim or perpetrator has staggered several miles, leaving blood traces around the neighbourhood, all of these drops will have to be photographed and catalogued.

The most challenging crimes to solve are those where the location of a discarded body is not the primary crime scene. Investigators then have to identify the victim (which could be made almost impossible if the body is incomplete or severely decomposed) and trace their last movements to the place where the death took place. One criminal profiler compared this scenario to finding the final page of a novel and then having to fill in the preceding chapters.

SEARCHING FOR CLUES

If a serious crime is committed in a busy street, investigators may have a limited time in which to gather their evidence. In such cases they may be forced to employ large search teams who will move in a line from one end of the street to the other to ensure they have covered every inch of ground. The same method will apply if there is a field or forest to be combed for evidence. Depending on their priorities, the seriousness of the crime and resources, the investigating officer may order a grid search which will require the search team to go over the same ground that they searched from right to left, but this time from top to bottom.

Any significant items that they come across will be indicated by a numbered marker and photographed so that a sketch or computer diagram can later be made of the area with all the significant clues flagged where they were found. Once an item has been bagged, labelled and logged it is impossible for someone to remove it or tamper with it. Fifty years ago evidence obtained

by the police and FBI was rarely questioned, but considered among the facts in the case. Now, in our more cynical age where corruption among law enforcement officers is a possibility and the credibility of expert witnesses and forensic science is routinely questioned, it has become necessary to prove that the evidence is genuine and has not been compromised.

If it is a rural location it is routine procedure to take a sample of soil in case it can be matched to trace evidence on the suspect's shoes or clothing which could place them at the scene. Finally, the CSIs' own overalls are examined in case they have inadvertently picked up any residual material.

If the crime took place at the victim's own home or place of business then the investigation team can employ fewer officers and take as long as they need to make a thorough search. In the case of the pipe bomb murder of Chris Marquis, for example (see 'Mail Order Murder' page 182), investigators were able to return to the scene several times until they eventually found the vital clue they needed. By contrast, in the Ty Lathon drive-by shooting (see 'Driven To Murder' page 70), there were few clues at the scene. The killer had taken the most significant clue with him on the wheels of his car. The mineral deposits at the scene were found to be unique to the area and were subsequently matched to those found in mud caked to the wheel rims of his jeep. In another highly unusual case, a resourceful police officer had the foresight to ask the mother of an abductee to vacuum her living room and then he archived the dust so that many years later forensic scientists could identify its contents and match it to microscopic paint particles in the killer's car.

It is unfortunate that so much time and effort has to be spent on what often turn out to be fruitless searches for evidence, but nothing can be allowed to be overlooked. It can take just one piece of incriminating evidence to crack killers' airtight alibis and convince a jury that they are guilty, no matter how confident and convincing they may appear during their day in court.

Members of the San Diego County Search Team perform a grid search near where a body was found

COLLECTING EVIDENCE

Contrary to the picture of crime scene investigators presented in procedural police series, forensic investigators are not concerned with solving the crime. The job of a CSI is to gather and analyze physical evidence so that the detectives assigned to the case can put the various pieces of the puzzle together and determine who did what to whom, where, when and why. A CSI is dedicated to revealing the truth with the impartiality of a technician and it may be that the truth is that there is no crime to investigate. What was thought to be a suspicious death sometimes turns out to have been a suicide or tragic accident.

An apparent case of arson may have been caused by faulty wiring or carelessness, such as a discarded match or cigarette, while an explosion might have been triggered by a gas leak or a series of unforeseen and otherwise unconnected coincidences.

Likewise, an apparent heart attack may be revealed to have been a poisoning, a drowning may be proven to have been deliberate and a tragic accident may be shown to have been an elaborate and callous attempt to defraud an insurance company. The only sure way of

Sherlock Holmes, the master of deductive reasoning

uncovering the truth in such circumstances is to maintain a clinical detachment from the evidence and let it tell its own story rather than trying to fit the evidence to a theory. This method of solving crime is known as deductive reasoning, the kind used by the most celebrated of fictional amateur sleuths Sherlock Holmes, Hercule Poirot, Miss Marple and many, many more.

But unlike Holmes and his fictional colleagues who were armed with little more than a magnifying glass and a chemistry set, today's crime scene investigators have a number of aids to determine the value of clues both in the laboratory and in the field.

A raging fire: deliberate or just carelessness?

CSI FIELD KIT

A typical CSI field kit would include the following:
- Protective suit to avoid contamination.
- Latex gloves. These serve two purposes: they ensure that the evidence does not become contaminated during transfer from the primary location to the lab and they also protect the crime scene personnel from the risk of biological contamination.
- Phenolphthalein. This chemical is used in the field as a presumptive test for blood to save time and lab resources. A cotton swab is moistened with one or two drops from a bottle of saline solution and then rolled against the stain to absorb the suspect substance. Phenolphthalein is added and, if it proves positive for blood, the cotton swab will change colour. The swab comes in a sealable plastic tube which ensures that when the cap is closed the sample cannot be contaminated.
- ALS (Alternate Light Source). This small pen-like torch is used to highlight faint fingerprints, biological fluid stains such as blood and semen and trace evidence including hairs and fibres. Its blue beam reflects back at a different wavelength than the light from a normal torch, requiring the attachment of a filter or goggles. In this sense it functions as a portable ultra-violet flashlight.
- Boots.
- Flashlight.
- Indelible ink marker pens.
- Measuring tape.
- Laser pens.
- Digital or 35mm film camera.
- Film.
- Tweezers.
- Evidence storage envelopes.
- Numbered plastic evidence markers.
- Flat rule markers for photographing significant items to scale, such as spent shell casings.
- Sketch pad.
- Blood drawing implements.
- DNA swabs.
- Evidence seals, tags, bags, and containers of varying sizes.

Chicago police use a ground penetrating radar device to check for the existence of buried bodies

In addition CSIs will carry kits for lifting fingerprints and making casts of footprints and tyre tracks, plus a standard tool kit for removing items such as door handles, bullets from the walls of buildings and so forth. They may also consider it prudent to bring a metal detector, a special vacuum with filters for collecting trace evidence and anti-putrification masks to avoid the noxious fumes and risk of infection when attending badly decomposing bodies.

Although these kits are supplied by the laboratory, some technicians augment it with household and hardware items they find particularly useful. There are also special kits for collecting bodily fluids, bugs, dried blood, gun shot residue and various hazardous materials.

A basic fingerprinting kit will contain:
- Ink pad.
- Aluminium fingerprint powder.
- Dusting brushes.
- Clear lifting tape and acetate sheets.
- Aerosol reagent to highlight faint prints and bloodstains.
- Magnifying lens.
- Scissors.
- Tweezers.
- Scalpel. These are supplied with sterile disposal blades so that biological stains can be removed without the risk of contamination. A semen stain on a bed sheet, for example, would be cut out and brought back as a swatch of fabric, while a flake of paint might be scraped from a car bumper that had been involved in a collision, or a smear of dried blood might be scratched off and placed in an envelope or plastic bindle to be brought back to the lab for further analysis.
- Gel lifters, for lifting hand- or footprints from hard, flat surfaces. Their adhesive backing is rolled or pressed over the print which can then be taken back to the lab and scanned into a computer for comparison with others on a national database.
- Electro Static Dust Print Lifters are used to lift foot, hand, palm and fingerprints left in dust or powder. An electrostatic charge attracts the powder to a clear sheet of thin film without disrupting the pattern.

A tyre and footprint casting kit will include:
- Casting powder and compound.
- Frames.
- Rubber lifters.
- Fixative.
- Wax spray to enable castings to be taken from snow.
- Mixing bowl and stirring implements

A laser trajectory kit, which enables investigators to trace the source and direction of bullets, will include:
- A laser pointer.
- An angle finder.
- Penetration rods.
- A centring cone
- A tripod.

A sexual assault kit, also known as a rape kit, will comprise:
- Evidence envelopes for pubic hair and fingernail scrapings.
- Swabs.
- Smear slides.
- Blood collection tubes.
- Pubic hair combs.
- Evidence seals with biohazard labels.
- Sexual assault incident and authorization forms.

ADDITIONAL EQUIPMENT
- Ground Penetrating Radar may look like an antiquated lawn mower but it is actually a very sophisticated and expensive piece of portable lab equipment which is rolled over an area of ground during the search for buried bodies. The signal penetrates the soil but bounces back when it strikes a solid object under the surface which will show up like an X-ray on the GPR's monitor.

Thermogram showing infrared radiation from the body of a murder victim

- The Bullard Thermal Imager detects residual heat on surfaces such as soft furnishings so that the impression of a person who recently sat in a chair, for example, can be photographed for later enhancement back at the lab. Using a thermal imager means that it is possible to determine the distinguishing physical features or characteristics of a person who has recently been at a crime scene, such as the passenger in a car in which the driver might have been shot and robbed. On the thermogram the areas of greatest heat appear light, while areas of disruption are dark.

- The Drager Tube detects and identifies several hundred gases such as toxic fumes at a suspected illegal drug factory.

- A Live Scan is a portable digital fingerprinting scanner which makes prints instantly available for comparison using a national database and does away with the need for the traditional ink and paper method. It is ideal for forensic work as it can be moved easily from place to place.

Footprints in fresh snow: trace evidence has to be gathered quickly before the snow melts

FORENSIC PROFILE: CRIME SCENE INVESTIGATOR

Deborah A. Hewitt is a forensic science supervisor at the Montana Department of Justice and a former consultant for the FBI. The most common question she is asked these days is not, 'Who did it?', but 'How can I become a CSI?' Her experience is that each laboratory will have different minimum qualifications for their forensic-scientist posts. Normally a four-year degree in a natural science (chemistry, biology, biochemistry, geology or forensic science) is the minimum requirement, with emphasis on chemistry and biology, and possibly a Master's degree or a PhD to add weight.

It is Deborah's experience that forensic science is becoming more diverse and highly specialized. In the 1990s a criminalist, as they were then called, would go on site to gather any evidence they considered relevant and analyze it themselves back at the lab, but today the courts demand a greater degree of technical knowledge so it is common for CSIs to specialize in tool marks, teeth, tyres, footwear, fibres, fingerprints, gunshot residue, gasoline or guns.

The first stage in analyzing a crime scene is to establish a workspace outside the perimeter to minimize the risk of contamination of the scene and to save time travelling from the location to the lab and back again. Points of entry and exit need to be protected so that investigators can avoid walking through these areas and evidence gathering needs to be prioritized so that transitory trace evidence such as footprints in snow can be taken before they melt.

A DEDICATED INVESTIGATOR

Deborah's speciality is footprints and fingerprints. The science of fingerprint analysis is more complicated than you might imagine. Prints are created by a composite of organic components

secreted by the person's own skin, mixed with anything else that they might have touched such as food grease, synthetic oils, paints, blood and so forth. Impressions have to be taken quickly; while prints made on smooth, hard surfaces can remain indefinitely if protected and undisturbed, those left on porous surfaces such as paper and wood can disappear quite rapidly because of the absorptive properties of the surface, although some have been retrieved from paper after 50 years.

When asked what sort of clues a CSI can derive from bloodstains, she will tell you that bloodstain-splatter analysis can provide a significant amount of information about a particular event depending on the patterns available and the condition of the scene and the evidence. Some facts that can be determined are the movement of the victim and suspect, the location of the blood source when a particular pattern was produced, the approximate number of blows sustained by a victim, the type of weapons used, the sequences of events, whether it is a primary or secondary scene, whether a victim has been moved after death and sometimes the time at which the crime took place.

Ask any CSI and they will tell you that the most difficult cases are not those that are traumatic, but those that are unsolved. Deborah admits that there is never enough money or manpower to handle all the criminal cases as fast as the investigators would like, but says that the most positive aspects of the job are being able to catch out a criminal in a lie and help to find justice for the victim. One might imagine that being a witness to the aftermath of so much violence could adversely affect the investigators, but they are given the opportunity to share their experiences during debriefing sessions and are routinely invited to private consultations with a counsellor.

PRESERVING EVIDENCE: FORENSIC PHOTOGRAPHY

There is more to forensic photography than simply pointing a camera at a dead body and clicking the shutter. The photographer's job is to record the

Indonesian police take forensic photographs at the site of a blast in Jakarta, 2005

scene as it appeared immediately after the crime was committed, with all the evidence in situ and undisturbed. It may be significant, for example, that a left-handed victim is found with their watch on their right hand as this would indicate that the body had been dressed after death, or that a male victim is found facing away from his murdered wife with his eyes and mouth sealed with masking tape as in the MacIvor murder case (see page 149). In that instance the photographs revealed that the wife and not the husband was the intended victim and that police should look for a sexual predator rather than a drug dealer as they had originally suspected.

Although crime scenes are routinely videotaped if there has been a fatality, sharply focused still photographs are needed to document the scene, the surroundings and the position of relevant items for both the investigative team and those involved in any subsequent trial where photographs will be entered as evidence.

As such they are vitally important in confirming or refuting a witness's testimony, illustrate a point the defence or prosecution may want to make to the jury, or establish that a scene may have been staged by the perpetrator, as in a recent case where a discarded school book had been planted by the supposed abductee to put investigators off his trail.

THE PHOTOGRAPHER'S DUTIES

The photographer will begin by taking wide-angle shots of the exterior with close-ups of any signs of forced entry. Next comes a series of establishing shots of the interior showing the general layout before close-ups are taken of relevant areas and individual items in each room such as discarded clothing, weapons and the position of bodies.

All individual items are photographed with a measuring rule to show scale. An assistant will keep a detailed record, including the camera settings, of every single shot that is taken, in case there is a dispute or discrepancy of any kind. It is only when the photographer has finished his or

her work that the bodies can be removed and the investigative team allowed in to look for evidence.

A forensic photographer has to be able to produce pictures of a consistently high quality as well as being able to adapt to difficult situations where there may be great pressure to work quickly, such as in a busy thoroughfare, or in a place where evidence is obscured by shadow. There is not going to be a second chance to photograph the scene once the rest of the team has been allowed to collect evidence.

Although digital cameras have obvious advantages over traditional 35mm film cameras, including the ability to enhance the image to draw out more detail, they are rarely used since images can too easily be manipulated.

The standard equipment is a 35mm single lens reflex camera, augmented by a tripod to guarantee rock-steady images when taking close-ups and a variety of filters and lenses for different situations. Filters and flash photography can create a 3D image to reveal the textured surface of tyre tracks and shoeprints or highlight bloodstains, fibres and gunshot residue.

THE PHILOSOPHY OF FORENSICS

Dr Jon J. Nordby, author of *Dead Reckoning: The Art of Forensic Detection*, is one of America's foremost forensic science consultants. A former medical investigator and philosophy student, Dr Nordby set up his own private company, Final Analysis, in the 1990s to offer forensic expertise and state-of-the-art laboratory facilities to overburdened and underfunded police departments on a freelance basis.

The key to criminalistics, he claims, is the ability to think clearly when faced with the daunting confusion of the average crime scene. That means relying on experience, intuition and abductive reasoning rather than text-book theories to identify what may be a clue and what can safely be disregarded. Abductive reasoning involves testing a likely scenario against the facts and only dropping it when one or more don't fit. It is the antithesis of

A stopped watch gives vital clues to the dramatic sequence of events that have led to a person's death

the traditional method favoured by most detectives, which encourages the investigator to assume facts from clues left at the scene and then to build the puzzle piece by piece, groping in the dark until the final piece is in place.

Abductive reasoning requires the CSI to visualize what the puzzle might be from the outset and then to see how many clues fit that picture. This means the CSI needs to be able to recognize the significance of specific items rather than making assumptions based on a perpetrator's previous behaviour or that of his personality type. Nordby believes that his approach helps recognize when a crime scene has been staged and keeps guessing to a minimum. It puts the clues in context and in doing so re-creates the true chain of events.

This new approach could soon be adopted by more CSIs because all too frequently investigators are being misled by false clues deliberately left at the scene by criminals who are now acutely aware of the importance of forensics and the significance of certain types of trace evidence.

FORENSIC PROFILE: THE CORONER

It is a popular myth that serious crimes are solved exclusively by detectives with the technical assistance of crime scene investigators and a pathologist who rarely emerges from the morgue. Although this team is the driving force behind many major investigations, there is a crucial member who is rarely credited with contributing to a case: the coroner (also known as the medical examiner). In Britain the coroner acts in a judicial capacity during the inquest to determine the cause of any suspicious or unexplained death and whether there is a criminal case to answer, but in America he or she has a more active role and frequently oversees the entire investigation.

Laura E. Santos, a deputy coroner with the Sacramento County Coroner's office, routinely attends the scenes of suspicious deaths. She interviews witnesses, researches the deceased's medical history, collates evidence and ultimately is the person who decides whether there is a case for detectives to investigate.

In California, coroners receive similar training to that of law-enforcement officers so that they are familiar with interview techniques and basic medical terminology and can interpret blood splatter patterns and other potentially significant clues as to the cause of death. They also need to have a basic understanding of anatomy and be up to date with common diseases and medications. However, despite impressions to the contrary, the vast majority of deaths investigated by the average coroner's office are from natural causes, with only 12 to 15 per cent attributable to suicide, accidents, drug overdoses and murder.

In 30 years Laura has learnt that each case is different and that the biggest danger is not a vengeful killer but complacency. Every death has to be treated with the same degree of inquisitiveness and a determination to uncover the facts. Even a natural death has to be examined if it was unexpected or if the individual had been suffering from a fatal illness and had not seen a doctor in recent weeks. In such cases the illness may be the result of poisoning, or even if was natural it may have been exacerbated by the wilful denial of medication, with or without the patient's consent. In cases of accidents there may be criminal charges to answer if the fatality was caused by another individual's negligence.

A case in point was the death of a 16-month-old child who had been declared dead on arrival in the emergency room of a local hospital from what appeared to have been natural causes. Despite the fact that the attending physician was satisfied there was nothing suspicious about the case, Laura insisted on treating it as an 'undetermined' death and ordered a routine autopsy. This revealed evidence of trauma and a homicide investigation was launched.

THE CORONER'S PROCEDURE

When Laura arrives at a location she has to determine whether the fatality is suspicious or not. Only then can it be declared a crime scene. The first thing she does is make a mental picture of the scene, securing an initial impression of the site and its surroundings, the position of the body and the behaviour of any witnesses, friends, family or neighbours which may prove relevant to her subsequent investigation.

While the CSIs collect and document any trace evidence, Laura will examine the body and make a preliminary assessment. An obvious sign of carbon-monoxide poisoning, for example, is unnaturally bright pink skin. Cardiac arrest produces a distinctive blue colouring of the upper chest and face known as cyanosis.

Laura will then examine the area around the body for prescription medicine and particularly empty bottles that may indicate suicide, assisted suicide or something more sinister. If there are what appear to be self-inflicted wounds, such as slashed wrists or gunshot wounds, is the situation consistent with what is known about the deceased? For example, if a gun is found in the victim's right hand and they are known to have been left-handed, there is the distinct possibility that it has been placed there by someone else.

An inventory of their personal possessions, including wallet, purse and credit cards, could point to robbery as a possible motive, although it is always possible that a scene may have been staged and the body posed to divert attention away from the real motive. An experienced coroner will be able to tell from just a cursory glance whether the scene is staged or not.

The next step is for the coroner to interview witnesses with particular attention paid to the person who claims to have discovered the body, as there is a possibility they might have been responsible for the death and be offering to assist the investigation so as to keep abreast of developments. Certain pathological types revel in being the centre of attention and being the key witness fulfils that role. If the witnesses are genuine they may provide important clues such as being able to confirm whether the doors and windows were locked. If not, the victim may have let the killer in, which suggests that they knew or trusted them – in which case they might be a family member, a neighbour or someone posing as an official such as an electricity meter reader.

Challenging cases

Laura's most challenging case involved a female serial killer who was convicted of murdering seven of her lodgers and burying them in the back yard of her Sacramento home. The drug-dependent landlady was convicted on DNA evidence after detectives were asked to trace the whereabouts of an elderly vagrant who had apparently vanished without trace. Fingerprints were of little use in identifying the buried victims as the bodies had badly decomposed in the decade since their death and, being elderly, many did not have their own teeth, which would normally have been an infallible clue in putting a name to the remains.

So Laura researched the social security records of everyone who had received benefits while living at that residence during the past decade. Thirteen couldn't be accounted for, so she requested their

X-rays from local hospitals and doctor's surgeries. A radiologist then made new X-rays of the bodies in positions which would match the borrowed X-rays from the patient's files so that any relevant fractures, deformities and distinctive features could be compared.

The whole process took nearly three months but meant that Laura was able to eliminate those who had died naturally or moved away. But not all cases can be solved and that is something that a coroner must learn to live with.

On another occasion Laura was called in to investigate the death of a teenager who had been found hanging in the back garden of his parents' house. His father had only been gone for a short while when the police were called in so it looked like a tragic accident, but by the time the parents began to voice doubts and suspicions it was too late for the coroner's office to pursue the matter as the forensic evidence had been compromised by handling and age.

Breaking the news of a loved one's death is another duty for the coroner and it is never an easy one, especially when it involves violence or the death of a child. She admits that it is often difficult to remain detatched from the more traumatic cases but she exercises and watches her diet to keep herself grounded. The average coroner's workload is not to be envied. Laura, for example, works four ten-hour days a week and is on call during all natural disasters and major accidents. But she admits that the work is never dull or routine and that she still gets a thrill out of riding in police motor launches and helicopters.

According to Laura the advent of DNA 'fingerprinting' has made identification of victims and suspects far easier and more reliable, but contrary to the impression given by TV crime series it is far from routine. Good old-fashioned fingerprints are still the most common method of identification, although it is only a matter of time before this too becomes computerized with all law enforcement offices having access to a national database such as the one featured on *CSI*.

case file

If The Glove Fits –
The O. J. Simpson Trial

The O. J. Simpson murder trial in 1995 was lost, as the prosecution would see it, through a combination of incompetence and carelessness on behalf of the Los Angeles police, who gave a textbook example of how not to process a crime scene.

The case against the former American football star and one-time TV actor was compelling. His ex-wife Nicole and her friend Ronald Goldman had been brutally murdered at her Brentwood home on the night of 12 June 1994, and there appeared to be indisputable physical evidence linking O. J. to the crime scene.

A bloodied glove found in the grounds appeared to match another recovered from O. J.'s house in Rockingham just five minutes' drive away, together with a sock which also had traces of Nicole's blood. Near the bodies detectives bagged a discarded hat which was later found to have hair and fibres which matched O. J.'s. And most compelling of all, there was a trail of bloody footprints leading away from the scene and bloodstains on the gate. The killer had evidently been wounded in the frenzied knife attack. When detectives called at O. J.'s home they noticed blood on a vehicle parked outside and a trail of blood from the car to the front door. Analysis proved that the blood on the glove found at O. J.'s home and the blood on the car were from three people, the two victims and O. J.

But O. J. couldn't be questioned. He had taken a flight to Chicago earlier that night and, when interviewed over the phone, appeared curiously uninterested in his ex-wife's death. On his return to LA the next day he was questioned by detectives, who commented on the fact that he had a bandage on his hand which he claimed was the result of having cut it accidentally on a glass in his hotel room.

He was allowed to remain at liberty for the next couple of days while the police concluded their examination of the crime scene, but on 15 June they lost patience with the star, who had gone into seclusion, and issued a warrant for his arrest. It was then that he attempted to evade capture during the now-famous slow-motion freeway chase which was televised live around the world.

It looked like the case against O. J. couldn't be lost. But it was.

O. J. Simpson looks at DNA 'autorads' showing the genetic markers of Simpson and the murder victims

POLICE FAILURES

O. J. hired a dream team of top-drawer defence attorneys who raised serious doubts as to the validity of the evidence, which they intimated might have been planted by over-eager or even racist detectives to frame their man. They even managed to secure a recording on which Detective Mark Fuhrman was heard to refer to Simpson as a 'nigger' no fewer than 41 times, which tainted the validity of his testimony and all the physical evidence he had accumulated. But the defence didn't have to work too hard. The police had undermined their own case.

On the night of the murder they had failed to secure the scene, allowing numerous personnel to trample through the bloody footprints and carry crucial trace evidence from room to room and out of the house on the soles of their shoes. Video footage of the police walk-through of the scene shows investigators working the scene without protective overalls or gloves and one policeman is actually seen to drop a swab then wipe it clean with his hands. During the trial Detective Philip Vannatrer proudly testified to the fact that old-school experienced officers of his generation did not wear protective clothing and evidently saw nothing wrong in handling evidence without gloves like a cop in a 1950s TV show.

The prosecution case was compromised still further by Vannatrer and his colleagues' insistence on going straight from the crime scene to O. J.'s home without changing their clothes or processing the evidence from the first location, which could have allowed transference of trace evidence from the crime scene to the second location.

And then there was the evidence which was captured on film by the police photographer, but which had not been logged in and could not be found in the archive. This included a bloody note seen in one particular shot near Nicole's head. It may have been irrelevant to the case, or it may have been crucial. We shall never know because it was presumably 'tidied away' with whatever else seemed like rubbish at the time and was lost. Incredibly, no photographs were taken inside the house, only of the immediate area where the bodies were found. So there is no record of any signs of a struggle or of any other relevant features or items that were later put back in their place.

ERROR UPON ERROR

More critically, the bodies of the victims were left as they lay for ten hours without being examined by a medical examiner, who would have been able to determine the time of death and recover vital trace evidence from the bodies. But after Nicole's body had been photographed someone had turned her over onto her back, eliminating the blood splatter that can be seen on her skin above her halter top in the official police photographs. It was the coroner's opinion that this splatter came from her assailant who had been injured in the attack, but no swabs were taken before she was turned. After she had been moved it was too late to do so. The coroner is also responsible for making a search of anything at the crime scene which might have a bearing on the cause and time of death. So a dish of melting ice cream

Blood covers the path outside the home of Nicole Brown Simpson

in Nicole's house which the police ignored might have provided a vital clue as to the time of death, but no one considered it worth photographing.

As if this catalogue of blunders were not enough to seriously compromise the prosecution case, the police also failed to bag the hands of the deceased, they neglected to use a rape kit, and they did not examine or photograph the back gate, which was the likely exit point for the killer. It was only weeks later that blood

Demonstrating the fatal stab wound in court

was found there, prompting accusations that it had been planted, when in all likelihood it had simply been yet another crucial clue that had been overlooked. These incredible errors and omissions were compounded after Nicole's body was removed to the morgue.

Instead of being examined in detail, it was washed, thereby eliminating the last vestiges of trace evidence that might have given a clue to the identity of her killer. It was only two full days later that an autopsy was performed.

After a protracted nine-month trial O. J. was predictably found not guilty. The jury could have done nothing else, since the police errors cast more than 'reasonable doubt' on the proceedings. But in a subsequent civil case brought by the families of Nicole Simpson and Ronald Goldman the circumstantial evidence was deemed to be overwhelming. O. J. was found guilty and ordered to pay $33 million compensation to the bereaved families.

Chapter 3
Material Witnesses

All criminals leave a trace at the crime scene, no matter how careful they might have been or how meticulously they planned their crime. It may be a single hair or fibre from their clothes, a partial fingerprint, the distinctive mark of the tool with which they forced entry into the property, the imprint of their tyre tracks or even microscopic flakes of skin. The challenge for the investigators is to identify which trace evidence is significant and which can be discarded. Equally valuable is the trace evidence that a perpetrator takes away from the scene, which on examination could place them at the location and tie them to the crime.

BLOODSTAINS

A dark stain is found at the scene of an abduction, but is it blood? If it is, it could mean that the victim has been injured and the authorities need to know that they are dealing with a ruthless kidnapper who may kill to avoid capture. Or perhaps the abductor was injured in a struggle and the stain could hold a vital clue as to their identity. DNA analysis is costly in terms of lab time and resources and every minute is crucial in abduction cases, but there are serology (bodily fluid) tests that can be done by a CSI at the scene which give instant results.

If an attempt has been made to scrub out a dark, incriminating stain, a single spray of luminol can reveal minute traces of blood which will glow in the dark as a result of the enzyme reacting with the chemical agent in the spray. Unfortunately, there are innocent substances such as potato which react in the same way, as they contain the same enzyme found in the haemoglobin molecules which distribute oxygen through the body in red blood cells. So a second on-site test is done which identifies whether it is human blood, animal blood or another substance with the same enzyme.

A saline-moistened swab is rolled over the stain and then sprayed with a synthetic (monoclonal) antibody such as Phenolphthalein which causes a specific reaction, turning the swab blue if it is positive for human blood. If it is human blood, the question is then whose blood is it? To answer that, a sample must be taken to the lab for analysis, but results can be speeded up by opting for a simplified antigen test which identifies the donor's blood type. Antigens are enzymes which provoke an immune response involving the creation of antibodies to fight infection. People with certain blood types will possess the corresponding antigens so if the victim is AB negative, for example, and the test reveals antigens associated with another blood type then it is extremely unlikely to be the victim's blood. The test is similar to that used to test for compatibility between patients and blood donors.

The most common blood type test is known as the ABO system, which reveals the presence of A- and B-type antigens. Two solutions of antibodies are added to the sample which forces the blood cells containing the A antigens to clump together, isolating the AB groups. The second solution splits the cells containing the B antigens from the AB groups. Blood type O is unaffected by the solution and so is easily identifiable as a group of distinctly separate cells.

BLOOD SPLATTER

It is usually only novelists, poets and historians that talk about blood being spilled or shed. Crime scene professionals know that blood rarely falls drop by drop to form a neat pool around a body but instead spurts from a wound in a gushing stream because of the pump action of the heart, leaving 'satellite splatter', 'spines', 'streaks', 'cast-offs', 'tadpoles' and 'transfer patterns' which to the untrained eye appear to be a sticky mess that speaks only of random violence and confusion. However, for the blood pattern analyst, splatter can be 'read' as easily as any painting, since droplets behave in the same way as projectiles and conform to the principles of ballistics. But unlike a bullet each drop of blood literally explodes on impact when it comes into contact with a flat surface and is distributed according to the velocity, volume, distance, direction and surface texture.

So splatter specialists are trained to recognize how blood will react when dropped and sprayed on every type of surface, including walls, floors, tiles, towels, glass, carpets and even the inside of a vehicle. Not only that but they need to be able to identify correctly the distinctive pattern made by various types of assault including hacking, beating, stabbing, sawing, slashing and cuts inflicted on an attacker in self-defence. They also need to work out how much force was applied as well as the relative position of the assailant to the victim, whether they were moving or stationary, at what speed they were moving and what happened immediately after the attack took place.

The many bloodstains at this crime scene provide vital evidence

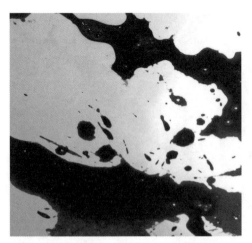

Each drop of blood literally explodes on impact

SPLATTER SCHOOL

CSIs are required to attend seminars and specialist courses just like every other professional, but at Professor Herbert Leon MacDonell's week-long basic blood-splatter seminar held each May in Corning, New York, forensic students and law enforcement officers vie for places as if they were front-row tickets for the Superbowl. MacDonell is acknowledged as the world's foremost authority on blood-pattern analysis and somewhat of a showman. His classes are highly theatrical but practical affairs in which the students are encouraged to dip their hands and various lethal implements in buckets of AB negative (supplied by the Red Cross) and imitate beating invisible subjects to death so as to capture the distinctive spray pattern on sheets of white card.

Professor MacDonell is a firm believer in learning from personal experience and there is nothing like creating your own crime scene to hammer home the specifics of blood-splatter science so you will remember it when you see a similar pattern on site. On one memorable occasion a volunteer was required to take a mouthful of warm blood and spray it onto a plain backdrop to simulate the pattern made by the last gasp of someone who had been shot. To the untrained eye blood sprayed on the shirt of someone attempting to help a gunshot suicide would be almost identical to that found on the shirt of a shooter who was up close to their victim, so the distinction is crucial.

Over the course of 14 key experiments the students learn everything there is to know about how blood behaves when it gushes from the human body by measuring its velocity, density and distribution. At the end of the week they will be able to look at dried droplets on a white card and say whether the victim was standing up, sitting, lying down or moving when struck, by what implement and from which direction. They will also be able to tell whether the victim was dragged or crawled to where they were found and if bloody footprints indicate whether the assailant was walking or running from the scene. All of this could be vital in establishing the perpetrator's state of mind at the time of the attack.

FOOTPRINTS AND TYRE TRACKS

Mass production and global distribution has ensured that millions of people now wear the same brand of footwear and drive vehicles of an identical make and model, factors that have significantly degraded the value of shoe prints and tyre tracks in criminal investigations.

Casts made from plaster of paris can help identify shoe prints and tyre tracks

Unless a shoe or tyre has a unique manufacturing flaw, features distinctive wear or carries trace evidence from the scene, its only value as evidence is likely to be circumstantial. Nevertheless, in an investigation every item of evidence is considered significant and treated as crucial to the case.

Even if the print is from a common brand of shoe with no distinguishing features, it can still be of help in building a profile of the perpetrator. Shoe size is roughly proportionate to physique; a small, narrow print would indicate a person of small build. And if investigators are lucky, the depth of the impression may reveal a specific physical characteristic such as a limp which could help narrow down the number of suspects, or the fact that the individual was carrying something heavy to the location where a body was found and returning with a lighter step, having been relieved of their burden.

Footprints found at the scene are routinely photographed using flash lighting to emphasize the depth of the tread with a measuring rule placed alongside the print so that a full-size enlargement can be used for comparison with shoes belonging to the suspect. The pattern made can then be copied onto clear acetate and overlaid onto the sole to see if there is a positive match. Impressions left in dust, dirt, fine soil or powder can be lifted like fingerprints with an adhesive gelatine on a fabric backing or with electrostatic foil. Alternatively, a cast may be taken.

To secure a cast the print is fixed with a hardening agent before the plaster or dental wax is poured in, after which it can then be scanned into the lab's computer, enhanced to reveal characteristic features and finally cross-checked against a footwear database to see if there might be a match to prints found at other crime scenes. Footwear databases such as SICAR are periodically updated by the manufacturers, who supply images of their new patterns because they readily acknowledge the value of the database to the law-enforcement authorities.

Tyre prints are photographed, fixed, lifted and identified in the same way. Once investigators have a cast or photographic enlargement they can identify the tread pattern using a standard industry reference guide that will provide the name of the manufacturer and even the factory where the tyre is made.

INDIVIDUALLY UNIQUE

Fingerprint analysis relies on the fact that every individual possesses a unique pattern of whorls, loops and arches on each finger which remain unaltered throughout our life and that each finger carries a minute residue of sweat to which dust and other microscopic matter adheres which is then transferred to whatever we touch. Although invisible to the naked eye these patterns can be highlighted by dusting with fingerprint powder, or

fuming with compounds such as ninhydrin or Super Glue which enables them to be 'lifted' on to adhesive film for analysis back at a crime lab. These are known as 'latent prints'. Prints left in blood or paint, for example, are able to be seen and are therefore known as 'visible prints', while prints that leave an impression in a pliable medium such as clay or food are classified as 'plastic prints'.

Prints can be taken from almost any surface, although the age of the print and the nature of the surface will determine whether it can be lifted at the scene or if the object needs to be removed to the lab, provided, of course, that it is portable. At the lab it will be placed in a vacuum metal deposition chamber which is filled with metallic vapour (first gold and then zinc) which adheres to the fatty deposits excreted from the finger.

For porous surfaces such as paper, standard fingerprint powder is of little use because the material will have absorbed most of the fatty residue from the fingers, so magnetic bristleless brushes are often used to powder the print with a fine dust of iron filings. Once the excess is blown away the pattern becomes visible and can then be lifted and photographed. Alternatively, chemical reagents can be used which change colour when in contact with sweat.

THE GREAT TRAIN ROBBERY

Today we are used to hearing of multi-million dollar heists such as the 1983 Brinks Mat Bullion Robbery at London's Heathrow Airport which netted £26 million in gold bullion and the recent £26.5 million Northern Bank raid when the finger of suspicion was pointed at the IRA. By contrast, the £2.3 million haul from the Great Train Robbery of 1963 might not seem so impressive (especially when it had to be shared among a large gang), but it was the sheer audacity of their exploit which caught the public imagination.

Nothing like it had been attempted in Britain before and, to add spice to the proceedings, some of the gang managed to escape to more exotic locales from where they thumbed their noses at the authorities who appeared powerless to extradite them.

But although they liked to think of themselves as lovable rogues, they were neither sophisticated nor smart. During the course of the robbery they had hit the driver over the head so severely that he was traumatised for the rest of his life. And when they fled from their safe house in Oxfordshire as the police closed in they hadn't the sense to wipe their fingerprints from the cups they had been using or from the playing pieces in the monopoly game which they had been playing with real money to while away the days spent in hiding.

Their prints on the bank notes used in the game linked them to the cash that had been taken from the train which wrapped up the case against them and ensured that the gang did not pass 'Go' but went directly to jail.

Bruce Richard Reynolds, the last of the great train robbers to be captured, arrives for a brief court appearance in 1968

EVALUATING PRINTS

Of course, investigators will only be able to come up with a match if the perpetrator's prints are in the national AFIS database (automated fingerprint identification systems) as the result of an earlier conviction, but in the US alone there are several hundred million prints on file and as many of these are career criminals who are likely to reoffend, the chance of obtaining a positive match is very high.

It takes the computer less than a second to evaluate a suspect's prints against a half million in the database by scanning the geometric pattern and comparing ten key points in the whorls, loops and ridges. But even when a match is made the technician must determine whether it is valid or not. He or she will be looking at four signature features: arches, which, as the term implies, are formed by ridges running from one side to the other with an arc in the centre; tented arches, which have a sharp point and are rare, seen in only about 5 per cent of the population; whorls, which take their name from an elliptical spiral pattern that evolves from a central point like a spring that has been pulled out of shape; and loops, which have a gentler curve than an arch, with the ends converging. Radial loops lean toward the thumb with ulnar loops slanting to the opposite side. For this reason it is crucial to record from which hand the print was taken.

Some people have what are known as 'accidentals' which create an irregular pattern. More rarely found are people whose prints are a

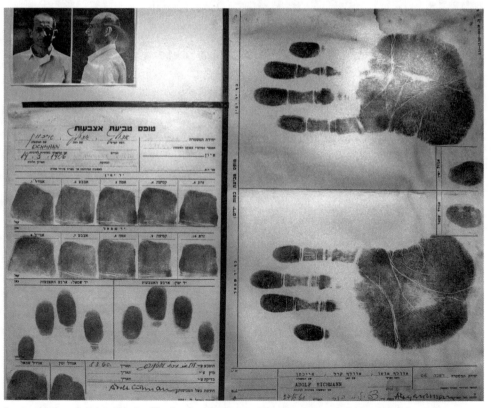

A reproduction of an Israeli police file showing the fingerprints of Nazi war criminal, Adolf Eichmann

mixture of two patterns which categorize these prints as 'composites'.

Even in these days of routine DNA analysis fingerprinting remains a vital element of crime detection. The real value of fingerprint evidence, aside from its ease of use, is that it is universally accepted by juries who know they can rely on such evidence to place a defendant at the scene of a crime.

FINGERPRINTS

In 1823 Professor Johannes Purkinje, a Prussian, classified fingerprints into the nine basic types and in doing so laid the foundation of modern forensic science. Prior to this convicted criminals were identified by their

body measurements according to a system devised by a French medical student, Louis-Adolphe Bertillon, which was both impractical and inconsistent. In fact, it was only by chance after a pair of black convicts with the same name and body measurements were found to have different fingerprints during an investigation in the US in 1903 that fingerprinting was finally accepted as a more reliable form of identification.

The two convicts looked like identical twins and only the papillary lines in their fingerprints could distinguish between them. If fate or chance had not brought them together in the same prison at the same time the case for fingerprinting might never have been proven.

INCRIMINATING TOOLMARKS

It is said that criminals unconsciously harbour a desire to be caught in order to unburden themselves of guilt. While that may be true of those killers with a conscience who have murdered in a fit of passion and are later haunted by remorse, it is certainly not applicable to the career

criminal, rapist, terrorist or serial killer who will all go to great lengths to cover their tracks. A professional burglar wears gloves as a matter of routine, serial rapists often mutilate their victims in an attempt to destroy DNA evidence, and cold-blooded killers who are wise to the value of forensic evidence may try to dispose of their victims by fire, burial or dismemberment rather than risk discovery. But even the most calculating and meticulous criminal can be traced and unmasked by the marks left by the tools of their trade. Every implement leaves its marks and so can be matched to the material it was applied to, whether these are chisel indentations on a wooden windowframe, plier striations on bomb-making components or the marks of hatchet teeth on human bone.

Although mass-produced tools may be identical when they leave the factory, they inevitably acquire unique gashes, scoring and irregularities through repeated use. And though toolmarks can be as distinctive as fingerprints they need to be found and preserved immediately after the crime has been committed, otherwise they may lose their value as evidence since the incriminating marks will be eradicated by further use.

Photographic evidence is often not sufficiently reliable to provide a positive match so either the object bearing the toolmark will be brought in to the lab for comparison or a cast will be made using forensic resin. In either case a comparison can then be made by using the suspect's tool on identical material and studying the striations on the original object with that of the lab sample, in a similar technique to that used in ballistics when comparing rifling markings on bullets and shell casings.

However, identifying characteristic patterns may not be enough to connect the suspect to the scene, so the next stage is to subject the implement to further microscopic analysis for trace evidence which may have adhered to the blades or parts of the tool which will have come into contact with material at the crime scene.

case file

The Stratton Brothers

In 1905 the practical value of fingerprinting, or dactyloscopy to give the technique its scientific name, had yet to be proven in a British court. Then on 27 March that year Scotland Yard's leading detective, Melville Macnaghten, was summoned to the site of a double murder which promised to provide the proof the police had been waiting for.

When Macnaghten arrived at the scene in a small paint shop in the London suburb of Deptford he found the body of the elderly owner in a pool of blood on the ground floor amid the debris of a violent robbery and his wife bludgeoned to death in an upstairs bedroom. The only witness was a milkman who had caught a fleeting glimpse of two men fleeing the scene. The taller man was dressed in a blue serge suit and bowler hat, while his companion sported a dark brown suit, cap and brown boots.

Fortunately, there were a couple of potentially significant clues: two home-made hoods which the murderers had discarded and a single smudged fingerprint on a cash box found under the old woman's bed. But during his questioning of the officers at the scene Macnaghten learnt that one of the constables had pushed the box out of the way when the stretcher-bearers came to remove the old woman's body. So he sent the box to the Yard's rudimentary laboratory for examination and ordered the officer to have his fingerprints taken along with the old man's apprentice and the victims themselves.

FINDING SOME SUSPECTS

The next morning Macnaghten was informed that the laboratory had been able to lift a clear thumbprint from the box and that it did not match the prints taken from the police officer, the apprentice or the victims. A laborious manual search of the 80,000 prints stored on cards in the Yard's fingerprint files also drew a blank. But Macnaghten was confident that all he had to do was apprehend all likely suspects and obtain a sample print for comparison.

In those early days of forensic detection many common villains were not as circumspect as they are today and openly bragged of their crimes in the mistaken belief that only an eye witness could convict them.

With that in mind, Macnaghten dispatched detectives to Deptford's drinking dens to mix with the locals and listen for any mention of likely candidates for the killings. By closing time he had the names of brothers Albert and Alfred Stratton.

When questioned, Albert's landlady revealed that she had found black stocking masks under her lodger's mattress, while Alfred's mistress, Hannah Cromarty, offered to inform on him if the police would promise to lock him up as she was in fear of her life from his continual physical abuse. Hannah confided to the police that Alfred had left her room through the window on the morning of the murder to avoid the risk of being seen by the other lodgers and that he had made her swear to lie about his whereabouts if she were to be questioned. She told the detectives that he had also disposed of his brown overcoat that day and dyed his brown shoes black.

That was enough to have the brothers arrested and brought before a magistrate who would decide if they should be held in custody while the case was made against them. Fortunately for Macnaghten, the magistrate was curious to test the reliability of the new technique. He ordered the brothers to be held for a week and their fingerprints taken for comparison with the sample obtained from the cashbox. It proved to be crucial, as neither the milkman nor Alfred's mistress were able or willing to testify in court.

The science of fingerprinting was so new that neither the judge nor the jury had even heard of it. Macnaghten would have to prove that it was reliable or risk losing the case. Scotland Yard's resident fingerprint expert, Chief Inspector Collins, made a compelling presentation using photographic enlargements and blackboard sketches to illustrate the indisputable similarities between the thumbprint lifted from the cashbox and that obtained from Alfred Stratton.

The defence team, who were clearly unfamiliar with the technique they were attempting to denigrate, attempted to plant doubts in the minds of the jury by pointing out minor discrepancies which Inspector Collins was able to explain as the insignificant imperfections caused by having to roll the inky thumb over the card. To prove his point he invited each member of the jury to have their thumbprints taken and, having done so, pointed to the same discrepancies in their prints. The fate of the Stratton brothers appeared to be sealed.

DISHONEST EXPERTS
But then the defence offered the testimony of two key experts who were prepared to prove the invalidity of fingerprinting as a forensic

science, one of whom was an advocate of the rival system of Bertillonage and the other Dr Henry Faulds, the man who for many years had claimed sole credit for inventing the technique of fingerprinting!

Under cross-examination Dr Faulds was exposed as a petty and vindictive man whose bitterness towards those who had adopted and developed his technique was so intense that he was prepared to renounce his own discovery out of pure spite. During questioning by his own lawyer Dr Faulds became so agitated at having to justify his validity as an expert witness that he lapsed into a sulk on the stand and refused to cooperate any further.

The final offensive against the adoption of the new technique came when Dr Garson, a once-enthusiastic advocate of the now discredited system of Bertillonage, took the stand. Dr Garson had in fact developed his own fingerprinting method as soon as he saw that Bertillonage was losing credibility, but when he realized that his own system was imperfect he covered his failings by blaming the theory rather than his inadequate application of it.

As the public gallery fell into a hushed expectant silence Prosecutor Richard Muir approached the man who appeared to be the last dissenter against the new science, brandishing a letter which he held aloft for all to see. Had Dr Garson written this letter, he asked, and in it had he not offered his services as an expert witness on the validity of fingerprinting to the prosecution? Had his offer been accepted would he now be testifying on oath as to the value of fingerprinting instead of denying it?

Dr Garson blustered and prevaricated but was cut short by the judge, who condemned him as an untrustworthy witness and ordered him to step down.

The case against the Stratton brothers and in favour of fingerprinting had been proven beyond reasonable doubt. The brothers were hanged and fingerprinting was soon being adopted throughout Europe and ultimately in every country in the world.

Even today after the discovery of DNA profiling, fingerprinting remains the single most reliable technique in forensic detection.

The Widow Accused

Occasionally the police are so keen to secure a conviction that they overlook the evidence – or lack of it, as in the case of Susie Mowbray, a Texan housewife, who faced life imprisonment for allegedly shooting her husband Bill to death while he lay in bed. Described by friends as a 'generous man', Bill was given to dramatic mood swings, compulsive spending and, at the time of his death, was up to his eyes in debt.

Bill Mowbray was a wealthy Cadillac dealer in Brownsville Texas. He died from a single gunshot wound while lying in bed and his wife Susie, who had been lying next to him, was swiftly accused of his murder. Professor Herbert MacDonell, an expert on human bloodstain evidence, was asked to examine the physical evidence for the prosecution.

The professor concluded that Susie would have had blood on her nightgown if she had fired the fatal shot, which had been from such close range that it had left a distinctive star-shape rupture in her husband's temple. There was back splatter on the headboard and the sheets, but stereomicroscopic examination of the white long-sleeved nightgown revealed no trace of blood. Susie simply would not have

had time to change her nightgown before her daughter came running into the room only a few seconds after hearing the shot.

This lack of evidence however did not deter the local prosecutors who insisted on proceeding with the trial and even enlisted the assistance of

Professor Herbert MacDonell, regarded as the world's leading expert on bloodstains

a second 'expert witness' who sprayed the garment with luminol and claimed it revealed invisible blood spots. MacDonell's report was suppressed by the prosecution and Susie was found guilty and sentenced to life imprisonment.

An appeals attorney working with Susie's son, Wade, got in touch with the professor six and a half years later. As MacDonnell had been convinced that the Bill's death was suicide and that the prosecution had buried his report about the evidence, he was happy to give his services for free. It was only on appeal that MacDonell was asked to testify and the original expert was discredited, which resulted in Susie's acquittal. But by then she had spent nine years in prison for a crime she did not commit.

The professor examining the evidence

Susie Mowbray: freed after nine years in prison

case file

The On-The-Ball Billionaire

Abduction is a traumatic experience. Kidnap victims who survive their ordeal rarely remember anything of value to detectives, but Oklahoma millionaire Charles Urschel proved to be a shrewd observer with a keener eye for forensic detail than most FBI recruits.

On a warm summer evening in 1933 Urschel was abducted from his front porch at gunpoint by two armed members of a gang led by Public Enemy Number One, Machine Gun Kelly. Fortunately for Urschel, Kelly was not the smartest gangster of the prohibition era. He hadn't even thought of looking up a photograph of his intended victim in a local newspaper. So when he and his accomplice surprised two elderly men at Urschel's home that night they had to drag both of them into their car as neither would identify which of them was the billionaire. Later, having rifled through their wallets, the gang tossed Urschel's friend from the car and sped off down the dirt road to their hideout across the state line.

Kidnapping was a federal offence and so experts from the FBI were swiftly on the scene, but even they had to admit that the chance of locating the gang's hideout in such a vast landscape was like finding a needle in a haystack. They advised Urschel's distraught wife to wait it out. Before long a ransom note was received demanding $200,000 in cash and this was accompanied by a letter in Urschel's handwriting proving that the demand was genuine and that he was still alive.

TAKING IT ALL IN

Urschel was not only alive, he was more actively involved in his own rescue than the FBI agents. Though blindfolded and bound, he made a mental note of every detail of his lengthy and uncomfortable drive through the night which might prove to be of use, if and when he was finally released. From the sound of the engine and the feel of the seats he identified the car as either a Buick or a Cadillac. That in itself would have been of little use, but when they later pulled in for gas he overheard one of the gang making conversation with the female pump attendant about local farming conditions and recalled her commenting that the crops thereabouts were 'all burned up'.

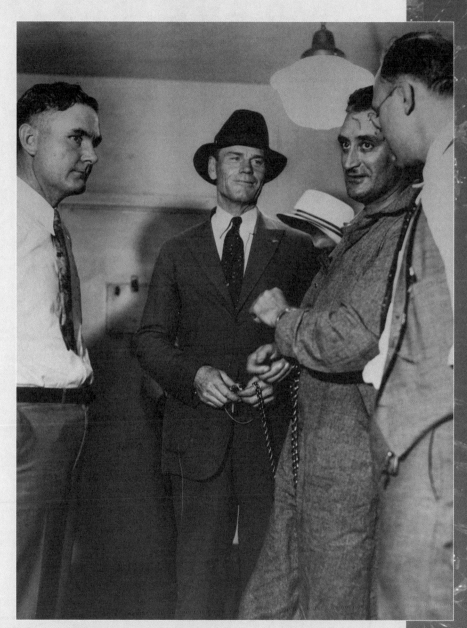

Prisoner in chains: a member of the gang who kidnapped Charles Urschel is captured

At the next stop he noted that one of the gang mentioned the time, 2.30pm. When they arrived at their destination Urschel was kept blindfolded, but he listened out for any sounds that might give away his location. It was clear from the barnyard noises that he was being kept on a farm and that it had a well with a creaking windlass.

More significantly, the water drawn from that well had a strong metallic taste from the high concentration of minerals. Kelly hadn't thought of removing his victim's wristwatch so Urschel was able to make a mental record of the time an aeroplane passed overhead, twice daily except on Sunday when a rainstorm presumably forced it to divert from its usual route.

By the time the ransom was paid and plans were being made to return him to his family, Urschel had managed to leave his fingerprints on everything he could touch. And thanks to the details Urschel had supplied, the FBI were able to identify both the aeroplane and the drought-affected area which it had avoided on that Sunday morning due to the storm. They contacted every airline that operated within a 600-mile radius of Oklahoma City and cross-checked schedules and flight plans until they had identified the flight that Urschel had noted. They pinpointed the farms the plane would have passed over at that time of the morning and again in the evening, which considerably reduced the number of haystacks they would now have to comb to find their needle. At the Shannon ranch they struck lucky. They not only found a member of the gang with his share of the ransom money, they also made a connection with the Kelly gang. They learned that Mr and Mrs Shannon's daughter Kathryn had married Kelly and even given him his nickname in the hope that the ham-fisted hoodlum who had never fired a gun in anger would be worthy of his reputation.

When Urschel was brought to the farm he immediately identified it as the place where he had been held. Even the water tasted as he had remembered. But most damning was the fine collection of his fingerprints over every surface he could reach which placed him at the scene, one of the few cases in which the victim's prints proved more significant than those of the criminals. Kelly was incarcerated in Leavenworth, where he died in 1954.

Law enforcement: Homer S. Cummings and J. Edgar Hoover plot the trail of the Kelly gang across state borders

case file

Geographical Forensics –
Driven to Murder

On the night of 26 September 2002 a fierce storm was raging through Front Royal, Virginia, making driving hazardous in this bleak rural district  **of Massachusetts. One driver returning home late slowed as he came to the flooded, aptly named Low Water Bridge and caught sight of something curious in his headlights. It was a vehicle with a man slumped at the wheel and another gravely wounded in the passenger seat. Both had been shot at close range. The passenger, 20-year-old Joe Kowaleski, was rushed to hospital where he remained in a coma for days, unable to give detectives the vital clues they needed if they were to catch the killer. His friend, Ty Lathon, was pronounced dead at the scene.**

When Kowaleski recovered he couldn't remember anything other than a glimpse of a red jeep approaching at speed followed by a blinding flash. More bad luck came with the realization that the rain had washed away all clues. All that remained were two empty 12-gauge shotgun shell casings and a set of skidmarks from a vehicle that had evidently pulled up alongside just long enough to allow a gunman to empty both barrels into the victims. However, it was impossible to take prints from the tyre tracks because they were on gravel. Both the weather and the environment were conspiring to keep the killer's identity a secret, but the motive at least was clear. There was an assortment of drug paraphernalia in the victim's vehicle and three cellphones, two of which belonged to the victims, the other owned by Lathon's ex-girlfriend Julie Grubbs.

Grubbs didn't own a red jeep, but her new boyfriend did. His name was Lewis Felts and he was a known drug dealer. Investigators staked out his home and arrested him when he appeared with a box of cleaning products looking intent on eliminating the remaining clues. They confiscated the vehicle and searched the apartment, where they found a significant quantity of drugs, $1,200 in cash together with a fourth cellphone.

Felts and Grubbs denied being at the scene, claiming to have stayed that night in Grubbs' apartment, 96km (60 miles) from the crime scene. But subsequent enquiries revealed that Grubbs had used the fourth phone to call Ty Lathon 22 times on the night of the murder and that her calls had been logged as being relayed from several towers along Route 50 as she had driven south. The final call was traced to Front Royal.

Although the cellphone records destroyed the couple's alibi they did not prove they had committed the murder or that they were at the murder scene, only in the vicinity. It was conceivable they might have been lying to avoid incriminating themselves in drug dealing.

THE FORENSIC PROOF

The detectives then called in a forensic geologist to examine dried mud found in the jeep's wheel wells. He sieved it to separate the coarser soil from the finer material and then subjected both to microscopic analysis. What he found sealed the guilt of the killer couple. In the samples of dried mud were fragments of sparkling blue azurite and emerald green malachite, copper-based minerals which had been washed downstream from a working quarry to Low Water Bridge. This discovery placed the jeep at the scene and all that remained was to place the weapon in Felts' hands. A friend of Felts came forward to tell how he had sold Felts a shotgun three weeks before the shooting. Better still, he had kept a couple of shells. These were shown to match those discarded at the scene. At the end of his trial Felts was found guilty of capital murder and attempted murder and sentenced to 25 years in prison.

What had appeared to be a drugs hit turned out to be an old-fashioned crime of passion. Lewis Felts had killed Ty Lathon over a girl.

Sometimes weather and environment conspire to protect the killer

case file

A Case Without A Corpse –
The Woodchip Killer

Forensic science is not simply a matter of running trace evidence through high-tech apparatus and printing out the perpetrator's ID after the database has produced a match. Even the most sophisticated equipment can only analyze the evidence. It takes a tenacious, imaginative and highly motivated CSI to gather all the elements, interpret the evidence and make a case. The following account is a good example of the lengths that forensic scientists must now go to and the attention to detail they need to secure a conviction.

Just before Christmas 1986, the police received a call from Keith Mayo a private investigator, who said he was concerned that his client, flight attendant Helle Crafts, had gone missing from her home in Connecticut. When questioned, her husband Richard claimed that she had stormed out after an argument and that he had no idea of her whereabouts. Neither had her colleagues, but without a body there was nothing much the police could do except conduct a routine missing persons enquiry. Until, that is, a snowplough driver remembered seeing a man fitting Richard Crafts' description operating a wood chipping machine by a river at 3.30am in the midst of a blizzard. The inference was clear. Crafts had dismembered his wife's body and shredded it into compost. If he had tipped the contents into the river the current would have distributed the remains across the state and no amount of circumstantial evidence would be enough to convict him.

Fortunately the coroner in charge of the case, Henry C. Lee, possessed local knowledge and told the police precisely which spot on the river to search as body parts had been washed up there in earlier cases. Sure enough, they pulled a chain saw from the water and were able to match it to the chipper and the truck that Crafts had rented. But even this proved only that Craft had discarded a rented saw in a river. It did not prove conclusively that he had mulched his wife's remains.

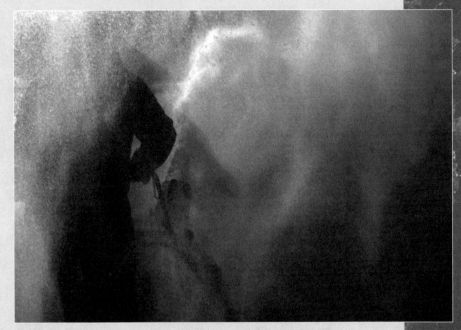

An observant snowplough driver's actions helped convict Helle Craft's killer

A GRUESOME TASK

So for nearly a month investigators scoured the first location where Craft had been seen using the shredder during the snow storm and were able to bring back a small mountain of wood chippings and what appeared to be human tissue to Lee's laboratory. There the team sifted through the debris, putting plant material to one side and human hair, tooth fragments and tissue in another.

Each hair had to be analyzed to see if it was animal or human and, if it was human, which race and gender it belonged to. Hair that had been pulled had to be separated from hair that had been shed naturally and then those that had been torn out had to be matched to a specific part of the body. Hair that had been cut had to be subjected to further examination to see if it had been cut cleanly by scissors or ragged by a shredder. After separating body fragments from the wood chippings, Lee and his team were left with just a few ounces of body parts, a fingernail, a dental crown, a bone fragment and pieces of plastic bag in which the body parts had been transported to the site.

Flight attendant Helle Crafts who went missing in 1986

Tooth fragments proved sufficient to positively identify the rest of the remains as belonging to the missing woman and when Dr Lee identified a bone fragment as part of the skull it proved conclusively that Mrs Crafts was dead. Moreover, the tissue on the chainsaw matched tissue found at the site; hair taken from Mrs Crafts' hairbrush was matched with hair recovered from the chippings and, if that wasn't enough, a sliver of nail polish was analyzed with a sample obtained from a bottle at the Crafts' house and found to be identical.

But the final flourish in Henry Lee's exemplary investigation was his decision to consult R. Bruce Hoadley, a forensic tree expert. By examining the chippings found at the river and those taken from the hire truck, Hoadley was able to state that they were from the same tree and that both chippings showed the distinctive cut marks made by the chipper that Crafts had hired.

If Richard Crafts had entertained hopes of evading arrest and prosecution for murder, he had seriously underestimated the dedication and dogged persistence of the forensic investigators on his case, who had spent almost three years putting their evidence together. When his case came to trial in 1989, Richard Crafts' defence was systematically demolished by Dr Lee and his team of expert witnesses. Crafts was found guilty and sentenced to 50 years in prison.

Private investigator Keith Mayo was hired by Helle Crafts before she disappeared when she discovered that her husband had had a series of extra-marital affairs

case file

The Battered Widow

When Leslie Harley, an elderly woman's nurse and companion, was put on trial for the attempted murder of widow Ellen Anderson in 1973, Harley's defence counsel claimed that the old woman's injuries were sustained during an accidental fall and that blood splatter on the ceiling was the result of Anderson shaking her head violently in response to her carer's questions and not of a frenzied attack with a poker as the widow had alleged.

But the defence underestimated the thorough and somewhat eccentric Professor MacDonell, who argued that even the most violent shaking of the head could not account for the spray pattern found on the ceiling of the old woman's bedroom. Even if the old woman had been able to shake her blood-soaked hair so violently that it sprayed onto the ceiling, it would have left a criss-cross pattern and not the perpendicular pattern found at the crime scene. When Harley's counsel came to cross-examine MacDonell he leaned intimidatingly close to the witness and sneered, 'Come now, professor, you have no basis for that opinion, have you? You certainly have never conducted experiments with a live subject whose hair was wet with blood to see how far they could shake it, have you?'

To the astonishment of the advocate and the court, Professor MacDonell proudly admitted that he had done just that only a few weeks earlier. Knowing that he would be called as an expert witness, MacDonell had replicated the incident by soaking a female volunteer's hair in human blood (an out-of-date batch obtained from the Red Cross) and had her lie on a table which was the same distance from the ceiling as the widow's bed had been. He then instructed her to shake her head violently from side to side and videotaped the results. As the professor had predicted, no blood reached the ceiling. But when MacDonell beat the pillow the volunteer had been lying on with a broom handle dipped in blood to replicate the poker he left the characteristic criss-cross spray pattern on the laboratory ceiling that the police had found above the bed at the crime scene. The video of the experiment was offered as evidence and Leslie Harley was subsequently found guilty and sent to prison.

Chapter 4
Crime Lab

Digital technology has transformed the traditional forensic lab. It is now possible to digitally reconstruct a crime scene so that investigators can determine the trajectory of bullets or recreate events that took place before police arrived on the scene. Computerised databases offer the chance to compare thousands of fingerprint, DNA and ballistic specimens and come up with a positive match within minutes. Using specialist software, forensic anthropologists can reconstruct a victim's face from their skull in a matter of hours, a process that used to take a skilled sculptor days to complete. Digital technology can also help recover vital clues from indistinct surveillance camera footage and from audio recordings, isolating crucial details that would otherwise have been lost.

TOUR OF THE CRIME LAB

A typical modern crime lab facility will include separate areas for DNA analysis, ballistics, trace elements and fingerprints plus a garage for stripping down vehicles, an evidence locker for storing items relating to a current investigation and a layout room for examining large items such as carpets, curtains and furniture. The latter doubles as a conference room where the team can meet to review evidence together.

THE DNA LAB

The DNA Laboratory is the heart of the modern crime lab. One microscopic sample of DNA can seal a suspect's fate, eliminating an individual from the investigation or giving the police sufficient cause for an arrest. Once a sample of DNA has been obtained from a suspect (either voluntarily or under court order), it can be compared to blood, hair, saliva or semen samples recovered from the crime scene.

To prepare the DNA for analysis the lab technician will put the sample in solution, using a micropipette which delivers precise amounts of the liquid agent. Then the sample is placed in a centrifuge which separates it into its component parts. If unidentified blood, saliva or ephithelial cells (skin fragments) are recovered they can be put through a ABI 310 Genetic analyzer to identify the genetic makeup of the owner. The resulting DNA profile can then be compared to the many thousands obtained from offenders on the CODIS (Combined DNA Index System) database in the hope of finding a match.

The typical modern crime lab is more functional and less glamorous than its television counterparts

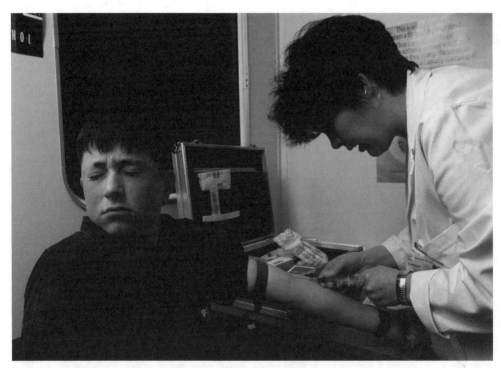

Until the advent of genetic fingerprinting paternity cases were determined using blood samples

DNA

Without a doubt, the most significant development in the evolution of forensic science was the discovery of genetic fingerprinting, or DNA profiling as it is more commonly called. Unfortunately, DNA analysis is not as fast a process as fictional crime shows would have us believe, nor can it distinguish between identical twins, but in all other respects the technique has armed law-enforcement agencies with a dependable tool for putting a name to otherwise unidentifiable human remains and placing suspects at a crime scene. And often from the smallest fragment of trace evidence – DNA can be taken from a single hair (provided that it still retains the root), a scraping of skin from under a victim's fingernails, a swab of saliva obtained from a suspect's mouth, a single drop of blood or a semen stain on the victim's clothes.

The discovery of DNA, the genetic code that determines human gender and physical characteristics, was made by two British scientists, Watson and Crick, in the 1950s. However, it wasn't until 1984 that another British scientist, Dr Alec Jeffreys, identified a series of repeated sequences within every strand of DNA that are unique to each individual, making it a far more practical system for identification than traditional fingerprinting. Initially it was seen as a significant development in helping to determine paternity suits which until that time had been resolved using blood tests which only indicated a probability of a biological link. DNA fingerprinting, however, could provide a definitive answer with odds of approximately three million to one that the sample would match someone other than the person profiled. At a single stroke the judicial system had a means of determining innocence or guilt in cases where there was 'reasonable doubt'. The discovery

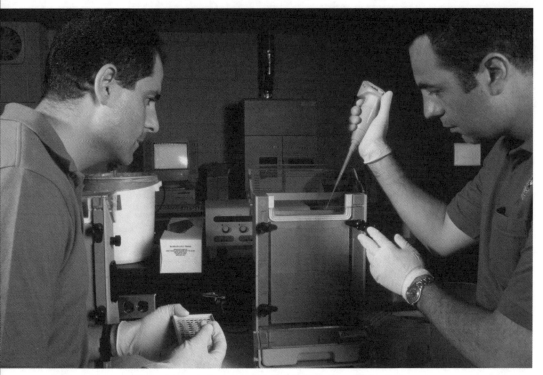

DNA samples are subjected to analysis to reveal their distinctive 'bar code' pattern

promised miscarriages of justice would be a thing of the past and decade-old cold cases would be solved provided the trace evidence had been preserved. However, its practical application had first to be proven in a court of law and accepted by the public.

WHAT IS DNA FINGERPRINTING?

DNA (deoxyribonucleic acid) is a genetic blueprint found inside the nucleus of every cell in our body and so is often referred to as the 'building block of life'.

DNA fingerprinting involves extracting a sample of DNA from bodily fluid such as blood, semen or urine, hair follicles, tissue samples or skin cells (known as epithelials) and analysing one particular region of the DNA strand known as STRs (Short Tandem Repeats) because it is only this section which determines individual, distinctive physical characteristics such as hair colour and facial features. The rest of the strand is concerned with more general genetic information common to all human beings.

STRs vary in length from person to person and, when treated with a radioactive probe, they produce an X-ray pattern similar to a barcode with a mixture of thick and thin black lines which can then be compared to those taken from a crime scene or a victim to ascertain whether they match. The process can be compared to scanning the same point in two different novels in the search for an identical sentence instead of having to read both books in their entirety to see how many times the same words recur.

DNA ANALYSIS

Inside the nucleus of each and every cell in the human body are 23 pairs of chromosomes made of deoxyribonucleic acid (DNA). Each DNA molecule contains four chemical units: Adenine (A), Guanine (G), Cytosine (C) and Thymine (T) which comprise its protein and enzyme elements and are paired in chromosomal strands known as a double-stranded helix which looks like a contorted ladder. DNA is coiled like a spring inside the cell, but if unwound each molecule of DNA would stretch almost to almost 1.8m (6ft) in length. The variations in the base sequence which determine our unique personal physical characteristics and our development are called polymorphisms because they vary from person to person. The unique 'bar code' created by the base pairs known as VNTRs (Variable Number of Tandem Repeats) makes it possible to make a genetic identification.

First the DNA has to be separated from protein and other material attached to it in a process known as extraction. There are two methods of achieving this. The first is called Restrictive Fragment Length Polymorphisms (RFLP) analysis, the second is Polymerase Chain Reaction, or PCR.

RFLP analysis

In RFLP analysis the extracted DNA is combined with a 'restriction enzyme' which breaks up the DNA strand into several components. These pieces are immersed in a gel to split the double-sided pieces into single strands. Then electrical current is applied (electrophoresis) which forces the negatively charged pieces to accelerate through the gel at varying rates toward the positive pole, thereby separating the strands according to size.

Using a nylon membrane, the fragments are lifted from the gel and are 'fixed' to the membrane with heat or allowed to dry. The four chemical components of each molecule (the A, T, C, and G bases of the strand) are now exposed and treated with a radioactive synthetic genetic probe made of a single strand of DNA. This is attracted to its complementary base; when it adheres to the base it forms a pattern which can be picked up using a sophisticated form of X-ray known as an autoradiograph and a print run off for comparison with 'bar code' strips sourced from other people.

Today it is becoming more common to use a chemical agent instead of radiation to illuminate the latent pattern, which takes only a matter of hours instead of days.

As with physical fingerprints, samples are matched using statistical probability meaning that a DNA sample with four identifiable fragments is statistically more reliable than a sample with three, but both can be of crucial importance in cracking a case. The chance of any two individuals sharing the same DNA can be as high as one in several billion, which means DNA can determine the outcome of a case far more effectively than conventional fingerprinting.

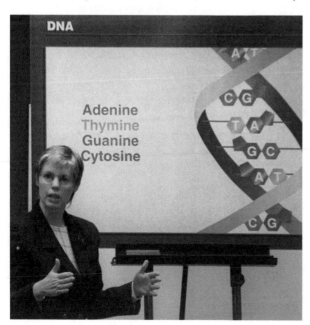

A DNA expert gives evidence in the O. J. Simpson case

DNA

Adenine
Thymine
Guanine
Cytosine

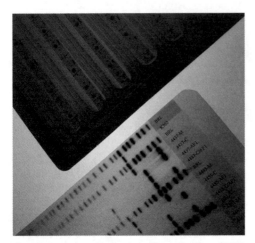

The PCR process replicates the cell's production of DNA

PCR analysis

The PCR process (also known as molecular xeroxing because it works by replicating the cell's production of DNA) is less precise, but it can produce valid results from a minute specimen, whereas RFLP requires a significantly larger sample for testing and if the sample is degraded it is unlikely to produce sufficient data to produce a positive match.

In the PCR process the extracted DNA is heated in a thermocycler which forces the elements to split into their component parts. The temperature is repeatedly altered and chemicals added to highlight a specific part of the DNA strand and make millions of copies which are known as amplified DNA. Then a typing protocol, or profile, identifies the distinctive lines of the genetic bar code so that a match can be made.

The success of DNA testing in America has resulted in the establishment of a central DNA data bank known as the National DNA Index System (NDIS), but the specimens are limited to specific categories of criminals who are compelled by law to donate samples in the belief that they are likely to reoffend or to have been responsible for previously unsolved cold cases which may be reopened in the future.

THE TRACE LAB

A single hair, fibre, scrap of fabric or sliver of paint can be enough to convict the guilty. By comparing trace evidence found at the scene with samples taken from the suspect, their vehicle or their home investigators can make a match using a Comparison Polarized Light Microscope that could prove conclusive in court.

For looking at objects in 3D and in fine detail investigators will use a stereo microscope. A good example of this would be if they were looking to match a roll of gaffer tape from the suspect's home with a strip of tape that had been used to gag a victim. The stereo microscope would reveal if the gag had been cut or torn from the roll recovered from the suspect.

If it is thought that there might be trace elements of drugs or explosives in material found at a scene it is possible to separate these for further analysis using a Gas Chromatograph Mass Spectrometer.

Cases that had baffled detectives for years have been finally solved by a new aid to detection known as an Infrared Micro Spectrophotometer, which analyzes the vibrational rate of compounds to identify their molecular structure. A few grains of soil scraped from a suspect's shoe or the tyre of a car can be enough to provide a molecular profile which then can be used by detectives to prove that their suspect was at the murder scene (see 'Driven To Murder' page 70).

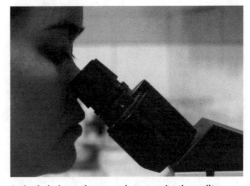

A single hair can be enough to convict the guilty

TRACE EVIDENCE – UNDER THE MICROSCOPE

The various types of microscope, now highly developed, have always been crucial in forensic science, bringing the guilty to justice by revealing evidence that is invisible without their aid. Identifying trace evidence may be taxing work, but it can provide the conclusive proof that nails down a case.

PAINT

To the naked eye a freshly spray-painted car might look brand new, but a thin scraping of paint examined under a powerful scanning electron microscope (SEM) can betray the fact that it has recently been resprayed to erase evidence of a hit-and-run incident.

An SEM is capable of magnifying the smallest measurable area, known as a nanometer, which is 100,000 times smaller than the width of a pin, to reveal multiple layers of paint and the order in which they were applied. Fortunately for forensic scientists, each manufacturer mixes their paint to specific formulae so that no two shades are exactly the same, although they may appear so to the naked eye. By subjecting samples from suspect vehicles to microspectrophotometry, which analyzes the wavelengths of light emitted and absorbed by a single fleck of paint, lab technicians can identify its chemical composition which will provide a positive match to a specific make and model and even name the year it rolled off the assembly line. From there it should be comparatively easy to find a positive match among the suspect vehicles and thereafter a thorough examination should provide more trace evidence such as clothes, fibres and blood to place the car at the crime scene.

Two British police forensic experts examine a car at the scene of a fatal stabbing

FIBRES

The typical crime scene will be littered with numerous fibres, some of which (such as cotton) may be too common to be useful to the CSI. But the trained eye will swiftly identify which strands to collect for analysis and back at the lab technicians will be able to separate synthetic from natural and animal hairs from human.

Forensic scentists can determine useful information about the race, sex and age of the owner of the human fibres. Having determined their origin, the lab technicians can then identify which part of the body a human hair came from, as the shape of each type varies significantly. The cross-section of a hair pulled from the head will be round, as opposed to a beard hair which is triangular and eyelashes which tend to be tapered.

Animal fibres vary in thickness but all have scales, which distinguish them from human hair. A burglar, for example, who leaves minute traces of dog hair at the scene after he brushes against the soft fabric of a curtain or sofa can be more easily traced once the breed of dog has been identified and matched to its owner. Killers have also been tracked down through plant fibres to specific locations where that particular specimen grows naturally or, in one case, where the perpetrator worked in a garden supplies centre. In such cases it might be necessary for investigators to consult a botanical expert.

Plant fibres have their own unique shapes and textures so that even after being chemically treated and dyed by the clothing or furniture manufacturer it is still relatively simple to identify them. Even the dye can be identified using microspectrophotometry or thin-layer chromatography (see page 87).

Synthetic fibres are more problematic as their method of manufacture means that they will all be uniformly regular, although texture, shape, solubility and chemical constituency should help to identify the manufacturer and from that the retail outlet where the item was purchased.

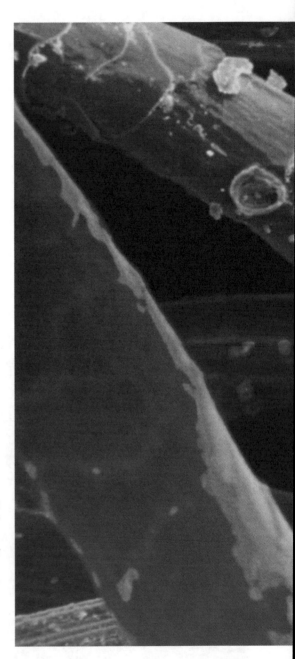

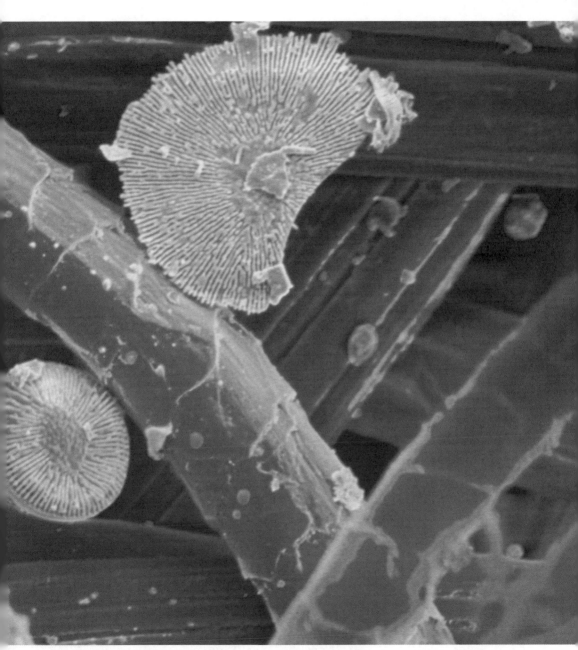

These diatoms (microscopic single-celled algae) were found on the clothing of a suspected burglar

GLASS

Similarly, glass may look smooth and featureless to the naked eye, but under the microscope each fragment reveals its distinctive density and structure which could lead investigators to the manufacturer and ultimately to the suspect. A thick pane of window glass, for example, will bend light to a different degree than a beer glass so it would be easy to determine whether a splinter of glass found on a suspect's clothing had come from a bar-room fight or from their work place, as they might have claimed. The refractive index (that is, the degree to which it bends light) of a sample shard of glass is measured either by a laser or by the traditional method of immersing it in a special oil which alters the refractive index when heated to a certain temperature. If the sample reacts to the heated oil at the same temperature as the glass found at the crime scene it is considered a positive match.

But even then the result needs to be confirmed by determining a second factor, the density of the glass. This is achieved by immersing the sample in two different liquids with different densities (such as water and liquid gelatin). Obviously even the smallest sliver of glass will sink in the former and float in the latter, so the lab technicians mix the two liquids until they have a solution in which the sample remains where it settles and this reveals the density of the glass.

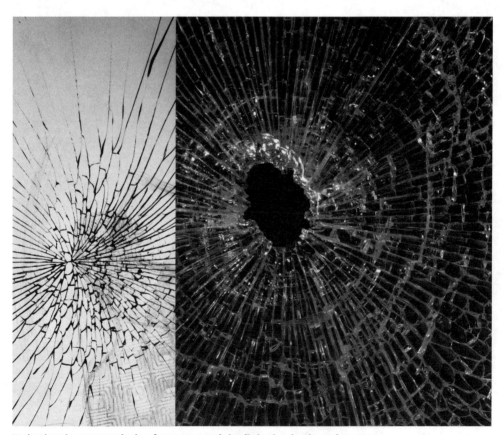

Under the microscope each glass fragment reveals its distinctive density and structure

TOXICOLOGY

The law makes a significant distinction between someone who accidentally causes the death of another person and an individual who causes a death while high on drugs or alcohol. Proving the presence of toxins in the blood of the accused is therefore crucial to the prosecution case. Both crimes are categorized as manslaughter, but the presence of an illegal amount of alcohol or drugs may prove either negligence or 'wilful disregard for human life' which would determine the severity of the sentence.

In Britain, police routinely administer a breathalyzer test at the roadside which measures the amount of alcohol in the moisture droplets contained in a driver's breath, but the results are not admissible in court. If the test proves positive a more detailed analysis will be made at the lab from a urine sample taken at the police station. A similar test for illegal drugs using an immunoassay kit can be administered to suspects once they are in custody. If there are chemicals in the urine they will cause a reaction when combined with the artificial antibodies in the kit, producing a colour change which indicates the presence of toxins. However, a more thorough lab test is necessary to determine what those toxins might be.

In the lab the presence of both drugs and alcohol is tested in the same way, using gas chromatography to isolate toxins from the natural chemicals contained in the urine. First the sample is vapourized and mixed with a neutral carrier gas (normally nitrogen) then passed through a perspex tube filled with granules which acts as a filter. The rate at which the constituent parts of the vapourized gas reach the sensor at the end of the tube is measured and their speed reveals the identity of the individual elements which are shown as peaks of various intensity on a digital graphic display. The gas chromatograph is usually augmented by a mass spectrometer which isolates the charged particles (ions), which can then be measured to create a spectrum which identifies their chemical composition.

Alternative methods include high-performance liquid chromatography, which requires a liquid carrier, and thin-layer chromatography, in which a specially coated glass sheet is dipped into a liquid sample of fluid obtained from the suspect which separates into its component parts as it is absorbed by the coating. These components can then be seen as a vertical line of discoloured spots creeping up the sheet in parallel to a control sample containing the drugs the lab are looking for. If the suspect's sample produces an identical pattern to the control sample, it proves the presence of the control drug.

POISON

Poison is a staple ingredient of classic Victorian crime fiction and a feature of many of the most notorious murder cases of the 19th century, but the lethal science did not go out of fashion with Hansom cabs and crinoline dresses. Even now jealous spouses and spurned lovers poison their partners, fatal drug overdoses (intentional and otherwise) claim dozens of lives a day around the world and occasionally multi-million dollar civil cases come before the courts alleging that irresponsible companies have poisoned innocent people by tipping toxic waste into drinking water, or burying it on landfill sites which are later bought for residential development.

Despite the advances in forensic technology the most reliable method for detecting the presence of poison in the human body is the traditional method, analysing a single strand of hair from the head of the victim. Not only will the test reveal the existence of fatal toxins but also the history of poisoning as indicated in the discoloured stripes along each strand, rather like the graded bands of coloured earth in geological samples.

Solvents and other hazardous chemicals will collect in the lungs while morphine, heroin and anti-depressants are likely to be detected in blood and liver, so if the coroner suspects suicide or an accidental overdose the pathologist will send samples of blood and bile to the lab for analysis using chromatography or the immunoassay method.

FIREARMS LAB

The most imposing piece of equipment in this department is the water tank into which bullets from a suspect's weapon are fired. The water slows the projectile and prevents it from being damaged as the unique rifling and striations marks must be preserved.

Bullets and shell casings recovered from a crime scene can be scanned into a computer provided that they are still intact. However, bullets embedded in walls and doors are usually too distorted or damaged to be identifiable.

If they are lucky enough to have a bullet or casing from the crime scene and another from the suspect's gun, investigators can make a direct comparison by placing them side by side under a comparison microscope to see if the striations match. If they match, then they know that both were fired from the same gun. Otherwise they have a chance of tracing the weapon by searching a ballistic database known as IBIS (Integrated Ballistics Imaging System) with which they can compare the distinctive markings on bullets and shell casings in the hope of finding a match.

Major crime labs carry a large stock of assorted firearms for reference. Most of these weapons will have been recovered from convicted criminals.

THE FINGERPRINT LAB

In allowing for a fast, on-the-spot treatment process, the Vacuum Metal Deposition Chamber is one of the most useful pieces of equipment in the fight against crime. If investigators suspect that there might be a fingerprint or palm print on an item that they can't lift a print from in the usual way, they can put the object in this machine. It sucks all the air out of the chamber, creating a vacuum, then coats the object in a fine layer of gold, revealing the pattern of the print.

Fingerprints which are not removable can instead be photographed then scanned into a computer to be compared with those registered on the database.

The water tank in a firearms lab helps CSIs identify if a particular gun was used in a crime

THE AUDIO-VISUAL LAB

Walk into any forensic AV lab and you could be forgiven for thinking you had wandered into a multi-million-dollar recording studio. State-of-the-art digital AV equipment has been a feature of film and TV post-production suites for decades, but since the early 1990s high-budgeted crime labs have acquired audio and visual recovery software in order to be able to enhance potentially significant details from low-quality surveillance cameras and to filter unwanted background noise from ransom tapes. Voice print programs are also occasionally used to isolate a criminal's voice pattern, which can then be displayed visually on a computer screen so that a comparison can be made with sound samples obtained from suspects in the hope of obtaining a good match.

Much of this digital technology currently in daily use by well-funded crime labs was originally developed by the aerospace industry. It has enabled investigators to recover images and identify voices that would have been impossible to salvage from analogue sources, but even digital technology has its limitations, one of these being the fact that every aspect of the technical process must be recorded in detail if it is to be admissible in court to ensure that it supports the facts and does not merely speculate on what might have happened.

VIDEO ENHANCEMENT

It is estimated that in major population areas the average person is captured on some form of surveillance equipment 20 times every day, which has led to security cameras becoming a prime source for tracking a suspect's movements. Unfortunately, most surveillance cameras are of poor quality, so to enhance the images forensic AV technicians utilize video enhancement software which filters out unwanted 'noise' and sharpens a selected area of the screen by filling in the missing or corrupted information which is distorting the image.

HUF Transform technology enables investigators not only to filter out corrupted data but also to manipulate a distorted section of the frame in order to bring out a specific detail. By calculating a rotation angle which will normalize the image when it is digitally distorted it can be viewed as if it had originally been photographed from this angle. In this way it is theoretically possible to read the number plate on a car parked at a skewed angle to the camera, or turn a suspect 180 degrees to see if he is carrying a rifle or an umbrella.

Vital clues can also be found in amateur footage, which is why whenever there is a major terrorist incident anywhere in the world the authorities issue a request for all tourist photographs and videos of the incident to be handed in for analysis. Obviously, there is a limit to the amount of detail that can be obtained during enlargement at high magnification even from digital data, especially when there is a low level of lighting or when the subject is moving, but it has been known to help investigators read a numberplate from a suspect's car caught on a speed camera and to catch the flash of a knife later thrown away by a killer who claimed not to have been armed during a fatal fight.

Digital also has the inherent problem of pixilation (the artefacts which comprise the image), which increases with each level of magnification, making the image look like a mosaic. But it is still a considerable improvement over the traditional method of photographic enlargement, which would produce a blurred image at a far lower level of magnification.

CRIME SCENE RECONSTRUCTION SOFTWARE

CSR software has been compared to the creation of a movie trailer where only the highlights are known and the details are left to the viewer's imagination. For a reconstruction to be valid, accurate measurements have to programmed into the computer so that various possible scenarios can be replayed until one is found that fits the facts and the scene as the police found it. If, for example, a man was found drowned in his backyard swimming pool fully clothed with a ladder lying nearby it could be assumed that he fell backwards while repairing something on the outside of his house, taking the ladder with him. CSR software would programme in his height, the distance from the body to the house, the length of the ladder, the angles and distances between each significant object and so forth. When the scene is replayed the man and the ladder should end up where they were found in real life. If not, then another scenario needs to be considered, such as the possibility that the scene was staged.

More commonly CSR is used in determining the train of events in fatal road accidents, where a vehicle's speed can be factored in using the thickness of the skid marks and the distance a second vehicle or body was found from the point of impact.

AUDIO ISOLATION AND RESTORATION

When an audio recording of a ransom demand or a threatening phone call is brought into the lab there are a number of processes it can be subjected to in order to isolate the caller's voice and also the background noise which may hold significant clues as to their location. If, for example, a recording has been made in a busy railway station the crucial voice or voices can be brought sharply into focus by rolling off the bass frequencies to eliminate unwanted

rumbling and booming from the passing trains. Reducing the high-end frequencies can also lessen the presence of background conversation which occupies the top end of the dynamic range and compression can be applied to push the desired voice to the foreground.

But these are not the only occasions when such specialized audio enhancement software might be used. A car caught on tape during a hit and run accident or a drive-by shooting, for example, could be identified from the engine noise although it would require a CSI with specialist knowledge to do so as there is currently no database from which to make a comparison.

Thanks to state-of-the-art digital audio technology, even damaged or partly erased data from an audio tape can be recovered so that a crucial conversation between two conspirators, for example, could be restored and used as evidence. The tape would be transferred to digital and the audio file cleaned up using filters which reduce hiss, rumbling and distortion. Then it could be treated with compression and equalization as described above to isolate and identify a particular voice or a sound.

A policeman secures a street as a body lies on the ground in Santa Monica, California

case file

A Scraping of Paint

In the 1950s London's traffic was considerably less chaotic than it is today, but even so pedestrians and cyclists could not afford to be complacent during the rush hour. After a female cyclist was hit and seriously injured by a careless motorist who failed to stop, police launched a city-wide search for the car. Witnesses described having seen a black Austin with the letters PN on the number plate speeding away, but there was little hope of tracking the driver down since it was a mass-produced model of a popular make and colour. But then police found a single flake of black paint on the bike's handlebar. This was subjected to microscopic analysis and shown to comprise four layers: two black and, below those, two green. Vaporized in a spectroscope, the flake produced an emission spectrum consistent with cellulose paint, the type used on motor vehicles of the period.

With no computer database to help shorten their search, detectives were forced to thumb through several thousand card index files in search of every Austin registered in the capital answering to the description. Nine were eventually identified and policemen on the beat were despatched to question the owners. All could prove that they were far from the scene at that time except for one, a man named Cameron who lived in Ealing and whose route home from work took him past the scene of the accident. While examining his car the constable noticed that the right wing had recently been retouched. The constable's suspicions were confirmed when he happened to see Cameron looking agitated in the mirror.

On closer inspection the constable found a few woollen strands stuck to the wing mirrors and took them back to the lab. Under the spectrophotometer these proved to be identical to those in the cardigan the cyclist had been wearing. More damning was a sample scraping of paint from the car which the spectroscope revealed to have the same composition as the flake taken from the handlebar. Faced with such incontrovertible evidence, Cameron admitted his guilt and was sentenced to three months in prison for failing to stop after an accident.

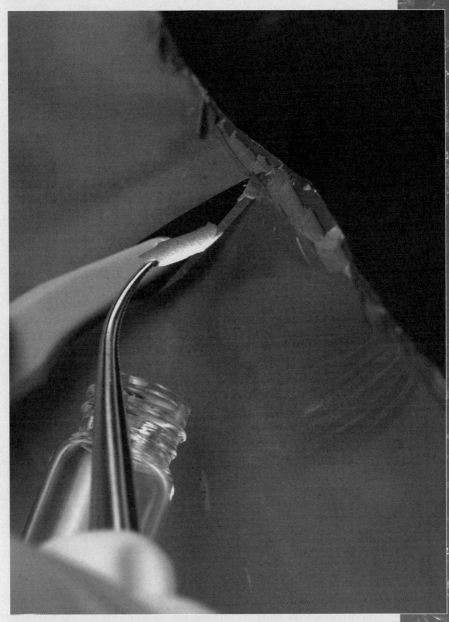

Tweezers extracting paint from a damaged car

case file

A Murdered Teenager

On the evening of 21 March 1962 Mr and Mrs Miller returned home to find that their 15-year-old daughter Marilyn had disappeared without a trace. Police searched the area and within hours found the girl's body face down in a reservoir behind the house. They also found footprints and tyre tracks on the dirt road nearby, together with a pair of discarded workman's gloves and a belt. No one in the neighbourhood had seen or heard anything unusual, although one of Marilyn's school friends remembered seeing a black and turquoise 1953 model Plymouth parked near the Miller house earlier that night.

The car was later found abandoned and inside was a pair of boots which matched the footprints on the dirt road. The boots were a lucky break for the detectives because they had been repaired using the heel from another pair of boots, which meant they produced a unique set of prints. Even more remarkably, the tyre was found to have a manufacturer's flaw which created highly distinctive tracks that matched the impressions found at the scene.

All the police had to do was trace the owner of the vehicle and they would have an open-and-shut case. Or so they thought.

The vehicle was registered to a local dairy worker, Booker T. Hillery Jnr, who had recently been released from prison where he had been serving time for rape. He was immediately arrested and charged with murder. During the course of the investigation the gloves were also identified as belonging to Hillery, which seemed to tie up the case for the prosecution and leave no room for reasonable doubt.

Hillery was convicted and sentenced to death. But the authorities had reckoned without Hillery's dogged determination to forestall the inevitable and an ironic twist of fate.

Through a succession of appeals Hillery managed to keep delaying the execution until 1974 when the US Supreme Court decided to abolish the death penalty. It was later reinstated but by then it was too late: Hillery's life sentence could not be revoked. Clearly Hillery was a shrewd and cunning killer whose sense of self-preservation outweighed any feelings of remorse.

Booker T. Hillery, right, is led into Kings County courtroom where he was convicted of the murder of 15-year-old Marilyn Miller

THE RETRIAL

In 1978, not content with escaping the electric chair, Hillery successfully filed for a retrial on the grounds that African-Americans had been deliberately excluded from serving on the Grand Jury in Kings County in 1962. It was a clever ploy because if Hillery could force a retrial he might be able to sow sufficient doubt to secure his release. Time had strengthened his hand. Of the original 24 witnesses, 21 were dead, and the forensic evidence could be disputed on the grounds that the tyre and boot tracks only proved that Hillery was in the vicinity of the Miller house. There was no irrefutable proof that he was actually inside their home. The date for a second trail was set and prosecutors had to present a convincing case or be prepared to drop the charge and see Hillery walk free – perhaps even sue the state for wrongful imprisonment. It was then that they had a lucky break.

But just before the case came to court, investigators discovered that a resourceful detective had asked Marilyn's mother to hoover her daughter's bedroom on the night of the murder in case there were microscopic trace elements which could prove vital in the case. These had miraculously survived in the police archive, and now this bag of dust and dirt was put under the microscope. It was found to contain tiny blue spherical paint particles of the kind produced by a spray can. Normally, when paint is sprayed on a flat surface, the particles flatten out, but these were round because they had been sprayed onto fabric. In fact, minute traces of cotton could be seen sticking to the paint.

On a hunch, detectives retrieved Hillery's clothes from the evidence store and found matching blue paint particles on his clothes that placed him at the scene on the night of the murder. They traced the paint to the interior of Hillery's car, which he had sprayed with this distinctive Prussian Blue pigment. Evidently minute particles had fallen onto him while he was driving and some of these were shaken off in his struggle with Marilyn. The irony is that Hillery had prevented the county from selling his car after the first trial in 1962 by threatening to sue them for disposing of his property, so it was still impounded 24 years later, a time capsule of perfectly preserved forensic evidence.

Twenty-five-year-old evidence had finally nailed a careless killer, and Hillery's bull-headed belligerence cost him another 25 years to life behind bars with no prospect of parole.

A Hair Out of Place

Even in the early days of forensic science it was recognised that a single strand of hair or fibre could contain enough evidence to convict the most cunning and calculating killer. The case of Johnny Fiorenza is a prime example.

In 1936 Nancy Titterton, a 33-year-old writer, was discovered dead in the New York apartment she shared with her husband, NBC executive Lewis Titterton. Her naked body had been found by two furniture delivery men lying face down in an empty bath with a pyjama jacket knotted round her throat and her underclothes scattered across the bedroom floor, indicating that the motive had been sexual.

On his first visit to the crime scene Assistant Chief Inspector John Lyons was optimistic of making an early arrest as the killer had been careless: in his haste to escape he had left behind part of a length of cord used to bind the victim's wrists, which might be traced back to him. Muddy footprints on the carpet were initially ignored, as a preliminary examination revealed that they contained traces of lint such as might be found in furniture manufacture and they were therefore attributed to the delivery men.

However, the search for the cord uncovered the fact that a New York wholesaler had sold a roll of it to the very same furniture store which had delivered a chair to Mrs Titterton on the afternoon of the murder. Then the city crime lab discovered an unusual hair on the bedspread where the rape had taken place. A microscopic examination revealed it to be horsehair of the type used in furniture upholstery.

As both delivery men had arrived at the apartment together Inspector Lyons assumed

Held firmly by two detectives, Johnny Fiorenza, centre, is led to the apartment in New York where the crime was re-enacted

that one of them must have gone there earlier; Mrs Titterton would have let him in as both men had visited the apartment on several previous occasions. When Lyons called at the furniture store he questioned the proprietor, who had been one of the two men to discover Mrs Titterton's body and who could account for his whereabouts on the morning of the murder. His assistant, however, had been absent from the shop and claimed to have been visiting his probation officer at the time. But, as Inspector Lyons discovered, the probation office was closed that morning for the Easter holiday.

When confronted with the evidence Johnny Fiorenza broke down and confessed. It seems likely that he placed Mrs Titterton in the bath not to revive her, but to cover himself in the event that he was caught when he would claim that her death had been an accident. But the judge and jury saw it as a cunning act of self-preservation and sent Fiorenza to the electric chair.

Faced with the evidence, Fiorenza confessed to the the murder of Nancy Titterton

The 24-year-old upholsterer's assistant, an ex-convict, in New York following his arrest

Doctor Double Cross

When 33-year-old Ohio paramedic Michelle Baker became pregnant, her live-in lover, soft-spoken and charming medical resident Maynard Muntzing, seemed genuinely delighted and offered to celebrate with a dream wedding on a tropical island paradise. But unbeknown to Michelle, Dr Muntzing secretly entertained hopes of being reunited with his former lover Tammy Erwin, and saw the baby as a hindrance to his love life. Nevertheless the couple flew to the island as planned, where Muntzing invented an excuse for postponing the ceremony. Michelle then began to suffer severe cramps and some light bleeding which she attributed to food poisoning or a local bug. On her return to Ohio she consulted her own doctor, who reassured her that nothing was amiss.

Michelle was initially delighted when Muntzing purchased a luxury home in which to raise his new family. But the cramps and bleeding continued, causing the expectant mother considerable anxiety. She then happened to hear a record request on her local radio station for a listener named Maynard whose voice was eerily familiar. Maynard was supposedly on vacation in Columbus at the time! Her curiosity aroused, Michelle drove to Tammy's home where she found her fiancé and his ex-girlfriend together.

A confrontation ensued, but Michelle was persuaded that the amorous doctor was committed to her and the baby and that his affection for Tammy was in the past. However, the nausea, cramps and bleeding continued, forcing Michelle to conclude she was being poisoned. She managed to smuggle a drink Maynard had made her to the police, whereupon it was proven to contain cytotec, a drug used to treat stomach ulcers which was expressly forbidden for pregnant women since it was likely to cause an abortion. But as detectives pointed out, there was no proof that Dr Muntzing had put it there; Michelle could have put it in her own drink to discredit her two-timing lover.

It was only when Michelle returned with a video she had made showing Dr Muntzing putting something in her drink that the police were forced to test her story. They too set up a secret camera in her kitchen which they monitored from the garage and thus they were witness to Muntzing mixing one of his mysterious cocktails while Michelle was out of the room.

They immediately rushed into the house and arrested Muntzing. The drink was analyzed and found to contain yet more cytotec. More vials of the drug were found in his car. Muntzing was charged with the attempted murder of an unborn baby, but the case never came to court. Unfortunately the prolonged, insidious poisoning had affected Michelle's health and just weeks before the trial she gave birth to a stillborn child.

Maynard cut a deal and spent five years in jail in addition to losing his medical license. He might still be there today had it not been for the fact that no cytotec was found in the placenta after the birth and Michelle's failing health meant that she was not able to take the witness stand during what might have been a lengthy trial.

Michelle Baker who was poisoned by her live-in lover

case file

Nicotine Poisoning

Suspicion comes naturally to crime scene investigators, who are trained to question everything – especially when there is a dead body at the scene and someone has benefited financially from the demise of the deceased. This is as true now as it was back in 1850, when Gustave Fougnies, the son of a wealthy Belgian apothecary, was found dead on the dining-room floor at his sister's house.

Gustave had been in poor health for many years and the recent amputation of a leg would normally have been considered a contributing factor to his early death. But the local magistrate was uneasy. Instead of taking on the pallid appearance of death, Gustave's corpse looked flushed and, on closer examination, his throat and mouth were found to have turned deep red as if they had been burnt.

The dead man's hosts, his sister Lydie and her husband Count Hyppolyte de Bocarme, were both deeply in debt and had been expecting to inherit her father's money until Gustave had announced his intention to marry, which would have left them with no prospect of paying off their creditors.

In due course the servants were questioned and described the curious events which followed the death of their guest. The Count had ordered a servant to bring a bottle of vinegar, which he emptied down the dead man's throat claiming that it would revive him. When it failed to do so, the Count had the body stripped and the clothes soaked in boiling water. More vinegar was summoned to wash the corpse and then the Count and Countess got down on their knees and scrubbed the dining-room floor.

The magistrate also learned that the Countess had served the meal herself, having first sent her children to eat in the nursery, which was unusual given that the dinner guest was their uncle.

ENTER THE EXPERT

A post-mortem was ordered and the stomach contents sent to Jean Servais Stas, a young chemistry professor in the capital. Stas was to become a seminal figure in the history of toxicology through his work on vegetable poisons. He immediately recognised that the vinegar was not strong enough to have caused the burning to the throat and mouth and so must have been used to disguise another more readily detectable toxin. By mixing the stomach contents in a solution of alcohol and then water Stas was able to filter out the foreign substance, which produced a distinctive acrid smell. It was nicotine, which in its pure state is a deadly poison comparable to prussic acid. Stas then mixed the dissolved nicotine with ether and allowed the ether to evaporate, leaving a flask of transparent oil which smelt and tasted of tobacco – enough to despatch several healthy men. The problem now was how to prove that it had been administered by the dead man's hosts.

The Count, it transpired, was something of an amateur chemist and possessed his own laboratory. He had gambled on the fact that vegetable poisons were undetectable, but he had reckoned without the indefatigable Stas, who was keen to solve that particular problem. Having distilled the colourless liquid from tobacco leaves the count had wrestled his brother-in-law to the ground and held him down while sister Lydie had poured the poison down her brother's throat. Traces of nicotine were subsequently found on the dining room floor. So strong had the liquid distillate been that even the scrubbing could not eliminate it entirely.

A deadly poison: amounts over 40mg can cause death

If the Count had intended the vinegar to mask the smell of the nicotine he failed. It was the acidic reaction of the two which caused the burns that had initially alerted the magistrate's suspicions. Moreover, when the vinegar was mixed with the alcohol in which the stomach contents had been preserved, it dissolved natural body substances leaving only the poison for Stas to distil. Ironically the Count, the amateur chemist who had used his knowledge for personal gain, had unwittingly discovered the formula for detecting vegetable poisons in the human body and had himself been detected by the one man capable of recognizing its potential.

case file

The Ghost Writer Caught on Tape

In 1971 rumours began circulating in the American media that eccentric billionaire industrialist Howard Hughes (subject of Martin Scorsese's Academy Award-winning movie *The Aviator*) had finally broken his 30-year silence to tell his life story to a comparatively unknown writer, Clifford Irving. Among Hughes' surviving friends surprise was mixed with incredulity and even suspicion that the story may have been a hoax since Hughes was a resolute recluse who had guarded his privacy as fiercely as he had protected himself from the germs he feared would infect him if he allowed contact with the outside world.

For decades he had remained in self-imposed exile on his palatial island paradise in the Bahamas, where he reputedly refused to have his hair cut or to trim his fingernails so that he now had the appearance of an ancient Chinese mandarin with waist-length hair and nails 20cm (8 inches) long.

Irving's publishers, McGraw-Hill, had reservations of their own, but these were allayed when Irving produced a sheaf of letters allegedly written by Hughes which were subsequently declared genuine by handwriting experts. There was not yet any book on Howard's life to which he contributed and this would be an amazing publishing coup if it was authentic.

Duly satisfied, McGraw-Hill agreed to an advance of $765,000 which was an unprecedented amount at the time, but the company was convinced that they had secured an international best-seller. They handed Irving a cheque made out to H.R. Hughes which the author promised to forward to the reclusive billionaire and they awaited delivery of the manuscript. Irving did not disappoint them. In due course he delivered a weighty 1,200-page biography which was eagerly read by Hughes' former associates who declared themselves satisfied that the memoirs were genuine. They had the authentic 'voice' of Hughes – at least they did so on paper.

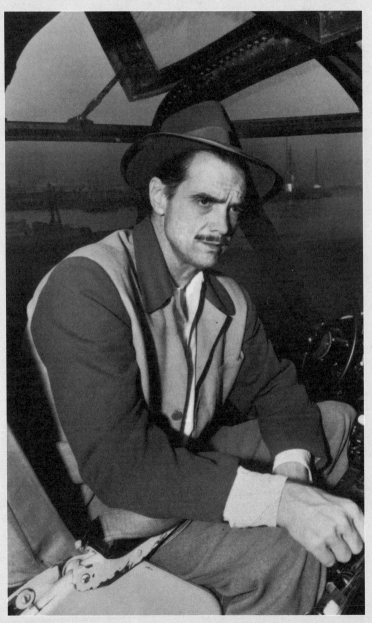

American industrialist, aviator and film producer Howard Hughes

VOICE OF A RECLUSE

Just as the presses were about to roll, associates of the billionaire announced that Hughes would be holding a teleconference at a Los Angeles hotel at which he would denounce Irving's biography as a work of 'fantastic fiction' and field questions from journalists who had known him in the early days.

During the two-hour session Hughes fielded a battery of probing enquiries which covered everything from technical details of the aeroplanes he had designed to trivial facts concerning the good luck charms given to him by female admirers. All were answered correctly. Then Hughes made a statement in which he denied collaborating with Irving or ever having met him. Furthermore, he wished it to be known that not a single cent of the $765,000 advance had been deposited in any of his many bank accounts. It was a convincing performance but there was still the question of whether the deep, resonant voice on the end of the phone line was genuine, or that of a well-informed impostor. There was only one way to find out.

Tapes of the conference were handed over to voiceprint analyst Lawrence Kersta, who compared the pitch, tone and intonation with an early recording of Hughes. Kersta's contention was that the underlying character of a person's voice remains constant even if the tone becomes frailer with age. After days of intense study Kersta declared himself to be convinced that the voice recorded at the teleconference was that of Hughes. But with a potential fortune at stake and the reputation of the publisher riding on the outcome it was decided that Kersta's verdict could not be considered conclusive, especially as he had a financial interest in the technology he had been using. The final word was then given to his fiercest critic, Dr Peter Ladefoged, professor of phonetics at UCLA, who had no vested interest in the outcome. Ladefoged subjected the tapes to detailed spectrographic analysis to compare the peaks and troughs of key consonants, vowels and phrases. He too announced that he was satisfied that the voice was that of Hughes.

The intense speculation surrounding the deal prompted Irving's Swiss bank to investigate the matter, after which they released a statement to the press confirming that a cheque for $650,000 had been deposited in the account of H. R. Hughes and then transferred to another in the name of Helga R. Hughes, Irving's wife.

Caught in a lie, Irving admitted his guilt and was sentenced to 30 months in prison. He was released after serving just 18 months and continued his career as a writer.

US writer, Clifford Irving, author of the fake Howard Hughes biography

case file

DNA Catches a Rapist and Murderer

The first true test of DNA fingerprinting came just three years after Dr Jeffrey discovered it, when police were investigating the rape and murder of two 15-year-old schoolgirls in the English Midlands. The first murder had occurred in November 1983, when schoolgirl Lynda Mann was found raped and strangled with her own scarf by a footpath in Narborough near Leicester. Fortunately, the police had enough foresight to preserve the semen stains, which revealed that the rapist was a Group A Secretor (someone whose blood type can be determined from other bodily fluids) with a pronounced phosphogluco-mutase (PGM) 1 + enzyme which is an identifying genetic marker.

But other than this they had no leads at all until July 1986, when another girl of the same age, Dawn Ashworth, was found raped and strangled 1.6km (1 mile) away from where the first victim had been discovered. A 17-year-old youth who had been seen in the area was questioned and charged. Under pressure he confessed and the police had no reason to believe that he was not telling the truth as he was able to tell them details that they believed only the killer could know. However, it transpired that he had chanced upon the body and so knew the murder scene at first hand and he shared the same blood type as the murderer, but he had not killed the victim.

Had it not been for the advent of genetic fingerprinting his presence near the scene at the time of the attack and his coerced confession might have been sufficient to convince a jury of his guilt and he would have spent the rest of his life behind bars. Fortunately, the police were aware of the radical new forensic technique and were willing to test it. They called on Dr Jeffreys, whose results caused consternation, as they showed Dawn and Lynda had indeed been raped by the same man but that the attacker could not have been the young man the police had charged. In fact, Dr Jeffreys carried out the test twice to ensure there could be no mistake. But that clearly wasn't the end of the matter.

Acting on the probability that the perpetrator was a local man, the police asked all men in the area of a certain age to donate a blood sample for testing. Every one obliged, but to the frustration of the police all 5,000 tests drew a blank. Either the test was not as conclusive as Dr Jeffreys had claimed, or someone had found a way to defraud the system. The future of DNA forensics lay in the balance until detectives received a phone call from a man informing them that a drinking partner of his had boasted that he had just given a blood sample to the Leicester police using another man's name. When interviewed, this individual, Ian Kelly, named the man who had paid him to give blood and said that he had only agreed because this 'friend' had convinced him that the police would stitch him up because he had a previous conviction for indecent exposure. The friend in question was one Colin Pitchfork.

After his arrest Pitchfork was required to give a blood sample which proved to be a perfect match with that of the rapist, but ironically he didn't wait for the result. Sensing the game was up, he confessed to both murders and subsequently received life imprisonment. His obliging friend, Ian Kelly, received an 18-month suspended sentence. But most significantly, the validity of genetic fingerprinting had been proven beyond reasonable doubt.

case file

Watergate

It wasn't the probing investigation undertaken by *Washington Post* reporters Woodward and Bernstein (played by Dustin Hoffman and Robert Redford in the movie *All The Presidents Men*) which led to the impeachment of US President Richard Nixon in 1974, but a single spool of cassette tape. Even as the high-ranking White House conspirators went down one by one like a row of dominoes, each accusing his immediate superior of ordering the crime and the subsequent cover-up, it looked as if Nixon might miraculously survive if members of his staff took the fall to preserve the Republican administration and what little was left of their leader's credibility. But then it became known that Nixon had ordered electronic bugging devices and voice-activated recording equipment to be planted in the Oval Office so that he could secretly record conversations with his own staff.

After much undignified haggling the beleaguered President was finally forced to hand over the tapes. To the dismay of his accusers nothing incriminating was found, although a lengthy segment was suspiciously silent during a conversation between Nixon and a senior White House aide. When questioned Nixon claimed that it had been accidentally erased. Undeterred investigators turned the tapes over to FBI forensic audio engineers who scrutinized the recordings for evidence that they had been doctored. Using comparatively primitive audio restoration techniques (which have since been superseded by digital software), the technicians discovered that the tape had been stopped and re-started 18 times, ruling out any chance that the record button might have been pressed accidentally. 'Tricky Dicky' had been caught out in a lie and was forced to leave the Oval Office under a cloud, narrowly avoiding imprisonment thanks to a pardon granted by his successor, Gerald Ford.

A Sharp-Eyed Investigator

Dr Edward O. Heinrich, one of America's foremost forensic scientists, was a man of uncommon abilities. His expertise in several different forensic disciplines together with his instinctive sense for deception helped him to crack two thousand cases and establish a reputation as the man who could make the evidence talk.

In the summer of 1925 Heinrich took delivery of the charred remains of a corpse said to be that of Californian businessman Charles Schwartz, whose case had been referred to Heinrich by the victim's insurance company. Schwartz had apparently died in a fire at his makeshift laboratory in Walnut Creek. However, the insurance company needed confirmation that the body was that of their client as Schwartz had taken out a life insurance policy just before his death for the staggering sum of $185,000 and his widow was unable to supply a single photograph of her late husband for identification purposes. It appears that her home had been burgled the day after his death and the photographs were the only items stolen. Undeterred, Heinrich contacted a photographer in Oakland who had made a portrait of Schwartz some months before and asked him to make a new print from the negative.

Once he had the photograph for comparison Heinrich knew that he was not looking at the corpse of Charles Schwartz. The man in the photograph had a mole on his earlobe which the body before him did not possess. Under the microscope strands of hair found at the scene were clearly unlike those recovered from a hairbrush supplied by the widow. During the autopsy Heinrich discovered that the dead man's stomach contents did not match the meal Mrs Schwartz had cooked for her husband shortly before his death and his eyes had been gouged out and his fingerprints obliterated with acid to make identification more difficult.

So, if the body wasn't that of Schwartz, who was it? A search of his premises revealed partially burnt fragments of paper with the name 'G. W. Barbe' and the words 'Amarillo, Texas'. Barbe was the surname of a preacher who had been befriended by Schwartz and given a job as laboratory assistant at the Walnut Creek premises where artificial silk was to be manufactured. The material Schwartz claimed to have manufactured the day before his death was revealed to be real silk and the so-called laboratory was nothing of the sort. There was neither running water nor gas and the electricity bills were too low for a working lab. As for the body, Heinrich learnt that Barbe was of a strikingly similar build to Schwartz, but three inches taller – the same height as the corpse. Barbe's eyes had been blue whereas Schwartz's eyes were brown, a discrepancy which would account for the mutilation.

Convinced that Schwartz was alive and guilty of the murder of Barbe the California police ordered local newspapers to publish details of the case. The landlord of an Oakland boarding house recognized the description of the arson 'victim' and called the police. When an officer called to question the lodger, he found he had taken his own life. And this time there was no mistake as to the identity of the body. It was Schwarz, who had left a written confession and a belated plea for forgiveness.

An artificial silk factory of the 1920s: Schwartz's own so-called laboratory was nothing of the sort

Chapter 5
Anatomy of a Murder

The body of a murder victim, or of an individual who has died in suspicious circumstances, is a crime scene in itself. A pathologist is called in to carry out an autopsy to determine the time and cause of death from a number of vital clues which are described in detail in the following pages. But there is more to the pathologist's role than merely performing autopsies. With their anatomical expertise and experience, they can play an active part in an investigation determining whether a death is due to natural causes, the result of an accident or was intentional – whether it was suicide or homicide.

DETERMINING CAUSE OF DEATH

The coroner, or medical examiner, is often a police doctor or an official with medical knowledge who attends the crime scene to make a preliminary appraisal as to the likely cause of death. The coroner is responsible for issuing the death certificate and ensuring that the manner of the deceased's passing is properly recorded. If the cause of death is manslaughter, murder or suspicious in any way, it is the job of the coroner to call in a pathologist who will carry out a post-mortem examination, or autopsy, to determine the exact cause of death (see page 118).

Pathologists only attend crime scenes when there has been a major incident they need to examine in person in order to understand the contributing factors to the particular injuries sustained by the victims. Coroners rarely become actively involved in an investigation, although in certain American states they may choose to do so if they are suitably qualified.

It is the coroner who will check for vital signs before pronouncing death by taking the pulse, listening for a heartbeat or seeing if blood is still circulating in the veins of the eyeball. Once this is done, there may be a need to strip the body of clues. For example, if there is ligature or bindings, these must be cut away without destroying the knots as the knot itself could be a signature of the killer or may provide a link to other crimes where victims were tied with the same knots or material.

When the coroner has finished the initial cursory examination and the photographer has recorded the position and location of the body, the scene of crime officer will cover the head, hands and feet of the corpse with clear polythene bags secured with tape. The body is then wrapped in a sheet, zipped into a body bag and taken to the morgue where it can be subjected to a thorough examination by a pathologist. Body bags are usually white, not black like those used in fictional TV series, as it is easier to see hairs and fibres against a white background.

If the amount of blood around the body is not consistent with the wound it is a sure sign that this is almost certainly not the primary crime scene and that there may be trace evidence in the suspect's vehicle if the corpse was transported from the primary scene to the present location. In this instance the coroner would have grounds for obtaining a search warrant for the suspect's home, place of business and vehicle in the expectation of securing vital physical trace evidence before it can be eradicated or contaminated.

DETERMINING TIME OF DEATH

Determining the time of death was once thought to be a vital element in a murder investigation, but it is very difficult to give an accurate estimate as body temperature and rigor mortis can be affected by several factors. The average corpse cools down by approximately one degree centigrade every hour but body mass, clothing and room temperature can affect this quite dramatically. A rectal thermometer reading is the most accurate method of recording core body temperature, but even this is prone to inaccuracy. Prescribed medication and narcotics can both affect circulation, which may lower body temperature, while the exertion involved in fending off an attacker or being pursued on foot for even a few minutes can bring on premature rigor mortis. Age is another factor. Elderly people and children often exhibit minimal signs of the tell-tale stiffening of the limbs, which can be broken by even the gentlest movement such as when a doctor might check for a pulse. Consequently, many coroners determine the time of death as being between the last time the person was seen alive and when their body was discovered.

Rigor mortis, a stiffening of the joints and muscles, usually sets in between 30 minutes and three hours after death, beginning with the eyelids and jaw. It affects the whole body in 6–12 hours, remains for a similar period unless it is disturbed and then dissipates over a similar period. Two days after death, bacteria in the lower abdomen will spread throughout the body to bring a green cast

First to the scene: it is the coroner's job to make the preliminary appraisal as to the probable cause of death

Within a week of death, the skin starts to turn white and the veins become particularly pronounced

to the skin, except in those who are uncommonly dark-skinned. Within a week the skin turns pale white with heavily pronounced veins, giving the corpse a translucent marbled appearance.

Another clue to time of death is lividity, or ligor mortis, a pinkness of the skin created when the blood settles after the heart fails and circulation stops. Lividity usually takes six hours to take full effect, and occurs on the body where it would naturally occur if a body remains undisturbed. So if a body is found lying on its back with a strong pink hue over the torso, it suggests the deceased was turned or moved to their present location after death.

FURTHER CLUES

The condition of the eyes is another standard determinate as death brings a fall in pressure of the fluid inside the eyeballs, which causes them to soften. After this a thin cloudy film develops in under three hours if the eyes are open, but longer if they are closed.

The chemical consistency of the body also changes after death, giving forensic investigators another variable to add to the equation. The potassium level in the eye increases substantially after death, creating a clear jelly-like substance in the eye socket known as vitreous humour.

Biochemical testing of this substance back at the laboratory can provide a fairly reliable estimate for the time of death.

If a corpse has been left to decompose for several weeks there may be work for an entomologist, whose knowledge of bugs can narrow the time of death down to within a day or two as insect infestation follows a predictable pattern (see 'Betrayed by Bugs' opposite).

Another fair indicator is provided by the stomach contents, which are examined during the autopsy as digestion can help to narrow the time frame as well as revealing what, if anything, the deceased ate in the last 24 hours of their life. Food normally remains in the stomach for up to three hours before passing into the small intestine, a narrow twisting tube through which it can take up to five hours to travel. So, if the small intestine is empty, it suggests that the deceased had not eaten for approximately eight hours, and if it is partially empty then it is likely that the deceased ate more than six hours prior to their death.

Even so, the pathologist must make allowances for other factors which can affect the rate of digestion such as anxiety, illness, alcohol and drugs, which can be factored into the equation once tissue and body fluid samples have been analyzed by a toxicologist

BETRAYED BY BUGS

Sadist and sociopath Alton Coleman carried out a series of brutal rapes and armed robberies across five states during the 1980s with the arrogance of a man who knew that even if he was captured he was unlikely to be convicted. The reason for his unshakeable confidence was that Alton could always rely on his retarded girlfriend, Debra Brown, to provide him with the perfect alibi. So when he was arrested yet again in July 1984, this time for the murder of nine-year-old Vernita Wheat, FBI investigators knew that they would have to provide incontrovertible proof that he was at the scene of the crime and not, as he would claim, with Brown.

Alton's fingerprints were recovered from the door of a derelict building in which Vernita's body had been found, but Alton could argue that he had been there on an earlier occasion before the body had been dumped. The FBI knew that they needed to place him at the scene precisely on the day of her death. The girl's body was too badly decomposed to contain any of the perpetrator's DNA, but the insects and larvae which had infested the corpse might provide a precise date for her murder.

Forensic entomologist Bernard Greenberg collected bluebottle cocoons which had been found at the scene and monitored their gestation process in his laboratory, having first collated 70 weather reports for the region to ensure that he could re-create the exact conditions the insects would have in Illinois at that time of the year. Normally bluebottles take 33 days to gestate from egg to adult at 15°C (59°F), but in Illinois in June the average daytime temperature rises to 25°C (77°F) which would have speeded up the life-cycle.

When the grubs hatched a month after the body had been discovered Greenberg was able to calculate the date the eggs had been laid to the early morning of 31 May, two days after Vernita had been seen leaving her home with Alton. Alton was tried, convicted and sentenced to death, but in a bizarre twist he was extradited and executed in another state for a different, unrelated murder.

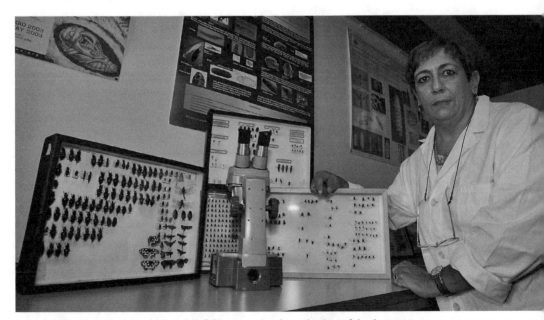

Forensic entomology: bugs can be very helpful in narrowing down the time of death

THE AUTOPSY

Most autopsy suites are functional, clinically sterile storage facilities which are usually situated in the basement of the local hospital with exposed pipes in the ceiling and a tiled floor for easy mopping up. There is a palpable chill in the air which is not entirely to do with the presence of death, but more to do with the need to maintain a temperature of 3°C (38°F) to slow down decomposition and arrest bacterial growth. But its most distinctive feature is the smell. It is one part preservative, two parts bleach and three parts putrescence. It can be strong enough to cause a medical student to pass out and is guaranteed to cling to your hair and clothes so that your family and friends will know where you've been.

If there are non-medical personnel present at an autopsy they will probably be grateful of the offer of a mask, but the coroner and his or her assistant will know that the odour can contain vital clues such as the faint scent of bitter almonds peculiar to strychnine poisoning and the sweet smell of

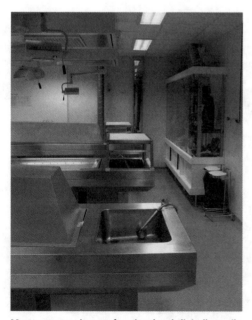

Most autopsy suites are functional and clinically sterile

ethanol, redolent of alcohol. The presence of liquor is particularly important to detect at an early stage of the investigation since, for example, intoxication is responsible for about 40 per cent of unnatural deaths in the US every year and it is not always detectable in the blood.

The smell of preservative, cleaning fluid and decay becomes stifling when the air conditioning is turned off during the trace evidence collection stage, but it is vital that no hairs or fibres are lost in the cooling air stream.

If the pathologist finds any potentially significant objects on the body, such as a piece of cotton wool stuck to a sock, he or she might ask the attending police officers to radio their colleagues back at the crime scene to see if more of that material was in the vicinity when the body was found. If not, it may have been left behind by the perpetrator, or may have come from their vehicle if the body had been transported from the primary location. This is because forensic science is based on a scientific law known as Locard's Exchange Principle which, simply put, states that, when two objects come into contact, there is an exchange of material. It is often microscopic and can occur when a person is struck by a vehicle or when two people are involved in a physical altercation. All the criminalist has to do is identify what was brought to the scene by the perpetrator and what they took from the scene or the deceased which will tie them to the crime.

Autopsies are compulsory in cases of unnatural death (that is, accident, suicide and homicide) or where the death is suspicious and 'unattended', meaning those where no qualified medical professionals were present to confirm the cause of death. Not all follow the procedure described here. A coroner may decide that only a partial or selective examination is needed in certain cases where the fatal injury is clearly evident (such as a gunshot wound or when confirmation of a previously documented disease or disorder is needed). In a partial autopsy the pathologist will examine the wound, whereas in a selective

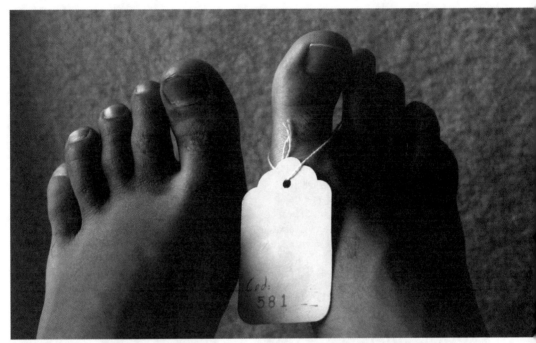

The body identified: an autopsy is compulsory in cases of unnatural death or where the death is suspicious

examination they will study a specific internal organ such as the heart or brain. The average autopsy takes an hour or two, but in more complex cases they can take days.

THE FIRST STAGES

Before the examination can begin the body must be photographed and undressed, with each layer of clothing being recorded by the photographer. If there is any significant trace evidence on the clothes or the corpse, this will be collected and catalogued by an attending CSI. If there is suspicion of sexual assault, the pathologist might scan the clothes and the body with an ultraviolet Woods Light to detect semen, which will appear as a purple-white glow.

The photographer will take shots of the body from all angles, paying particular attention to tattoos (see p122), distinguishing birthmarks, bruises, scars and wounds. He or she stays during the examination and records each significant stage on film. Each wound is measured and photographed against a grey forensic ruler which acts as a colour code to ensure that the photographs are developed with accurate natural colours as the colour of wounds and bruises is a reliable indicator of when the injury occurred.

A laboratory technician will then take swabs from the mouth, rectum and sexual organs as well as samples of hair for DNA analysis to aid identification if it is in question, but also to test for trace elements of drugs and poisons. Scrapings from under the fingernails might also be preserved if the deceased was a victim of an assault and then the hands are swabbed for gunpowder residue if appropriate and the deceased's fingerprints are taken, although this can be difficult if the body is in an advanced state of decomposition. Even in the recently deceased the veins in the hands protrude, making fingerprinting awkward. The top layer of skin may also be exhibiting slippage (slackening) and can peel away if not handled with care.

The body is then washed and replaced on the metallic dissection table which is perforated with drainage holes and has a surrounding ridge to retain body fluids. A second tier acts as a basin, catching all fluids which are continually rinsed away by a pump. A hanging scale at the foot of the table is used for weighing individual organs, after which they are placed on a small steel side table with a corkboard cutting block for dissection. Nearby there will be a selection of sample jars filled with formalin preservative and a range of formidable-looking dissecting tools which bear little resemblance to the small precision surgical implements used in the operating theatres on the upper floors.

The body bag and clothing are then packed, labelled and sent for further analysis.

If there are knife or bullet wounds the pathologist will trace their trajectory with dowelling rods and record the results. He or she may also take X-rays of any wounds, because once the autopsy has been completed the body can be released for burial, although in very unusual cases it may be disinterred at a later date or subjected to a second autopsy if the first proves inconclusive, as in the case of the mysterious death of millionaire Robert Maxwell (see page 127).

The pathologist begins the internal examination by dissecting the torso from shoulder to shoulder and down to the abdomen with what is known as a 'Y' incision to expose the organs. Using bone cutters, he or she cuts through the ribs and removes the chest plate, followed by the heart, lungs, trachea and oesophagus. Samples of tissue and fluid from these organs are taken and stored in a refrigerator for later analysis. Next, the

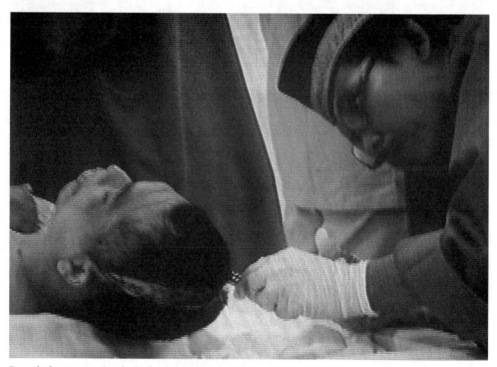

Forensic doctors examine the body of a slain bomb-maker in Indonesia

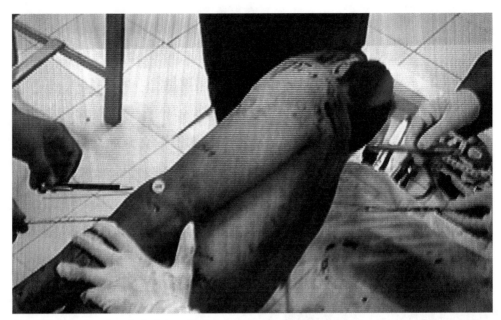

Exit wound: the direction of a bullet can be determined at the autopsy

abdominal organs are removed and the stomach contents systematically examined. Again, samples are bottled, labelled and stored in the refrigerator for future analysis.

Finally, an incision is made at the back of the head from ear to ear and the skin is peeled back, exposing the skull.

Using a stainless steel saw and cranium chisel, the skull is opened and the brain removed for weighing and for tissue samples to be taken.

ANALYZING THE WOUNDS

In cases of murder, manslaughter, suspected suicide or fatal accident, the primary crime scene is the body itself. Each wound, burn, bruise and abrasion can reveal how the deceased met their death, what weapon, if any, was used and ultimately, who was responsible.

A gun fired at extremely close range, for example, will leave a burn surrounding the wound suggesting suicide, a professional hit or a shooting with a very personal motive where the killer needed to come face to face with his victim. And unless the calibre of the bullet is extremely small, such as a .22, it will create an exit wound which will enable the pathologist and ballistics expert to trace the trajectory and so determine the location of the shooter which can be crucial if, for example, an innocent bystander is caught in the crossfire between police and criminals who are using similar weapons and the bullet cannot be recovered. Or, as in the case of the 1984 London Libyan Embassy siege, proof was needed that a fatal shot came from within the building and not, as was claimed, from the roof (see page 172).

In the case of a fatal stabbing it may be necessary to prove that the attack was malicious and not an accident as the defendant might claim. Sharp cuts on the hands of the deceased are likely to be defensive wounds as the victim attempted to fend off their attacker. An examination of the shape and depth of the wound can reveal if it was a frenzied attack, as well as the size and type of blade (sharp or serrated, single or double-edged).

A fatal beating with a blunt-edged weapon, fists or feet will leave characteristic bruises known as contusions where the blood vessels were ruptured by force. Although bruising continues to occur after death, the shape of the contusions can reveal the nature of the weapon, the direction from which the blows came and an approximate time when the injuries occurred as they change from red through purple, brown and green to yellow within a few days.

Some fatal injuries, such as a blow to the head with a fist and shaken baby syndrome, leave almost no external marks of any kind, but are usually detected during an internal examination when blood clots in the skull turn out to reveal a brain haemorrhage (internal bleeding) as the cause of death.

Murder by fatal injection is, fortunately, rare and very difficult to detect as the hypodermic needle will leave only a tiny hole which can easily be overlooked. But in such cases a trace of the poison or drug may be detected by the toxicologist's analysis of the blood sample.

As forensic tools and techniques becoming increasingly sophisticated it is easier to distinguish between a suspicious death and one brought about by natural causes. Before the development of histology (the scientific analysis of microscopic slivers of body tissue) circumstantial evidence was often sufficient to secure a conviction and send many innocent people to prison or their execution if it was suspected that they might have hastened the departure of a wealthy relative or rival. But now high-magnification devices such as a microtome can shave off a thin sliver of tissue from the vital organ under examination after which it can be stained with chemicals disclosing any damage caused by disease which may not have manifested as physical symptoms.

TATTOOS

When a body is found without any form of ID, there are no grieving relatives or friends to claim the corpse and even the police have failed to find a match for the fingerprints on the national database, there is one clue which can put a name and a history to the deceased. A good pathologist or police officer can read a tattoo as readily as they can a bullet wound. Armed forces personnel have their own brand, often inscribed with their rank and service number, which makes an ID only a matter of a phone call. Prisoners carry theirs with equal pride – a cobweb design or a clock without hands denotes a seasoned ex-con, while many Hispanic prisoners will have had a Madonna de Guadalupe emblazoned on their back to deter rapists. Other 'inks' can be used to camouflage a history of heroin injections or to boast membership of a specific street gang, an Aryan supremacist group and many other brotherhoods and secret societies. Each street tattoo artist has their own distinctive style and signature which makes tracing the tattooist time-consuming but frequently

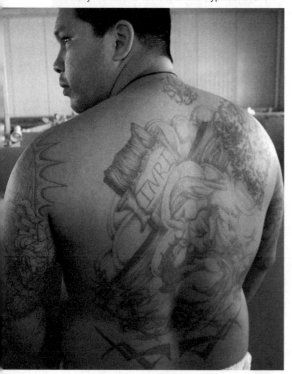

A tattoo can be traced as easily as a bullet wound

worthwhile, but the toughest 'tats' to trace are those done inside prison by the con themselves or their cell mate which are made freehand with ink or cigarette ash or by a home-made machine using an empty pen, a guitar string and India ink.

IN SUSPICIOUS CIRCUMSTANCES – CLUES TO MISADVENTURE

A young man is found hanging by the neck from a noose in his apartment, a chair lying on its side on the floor beneath his body. But was it suicide, or has the scene been staged to cover up a homicide? In such cases it is impossible to be absolutely certain until an autopsy can reveal the true cause of death.

If the skin has a blue cast and the autopsy reveals distension of the lungs and burst blood vessels in the eyes then death is due to a lack of oxygen (hypoxia). But this does not indicate whether it was caused by manual strangulation or a rope. A rope will leave friction burns which only occur when the individual is alive at the moment of strangulation, but these could be caused by a ligature. Unless there is a V-shaped abrasion around the neck created by the rope during suspension of the body, the hanging could have been staged after death. If the deceased does not have friction burns around the neck then he or she must have been dead before the rope was put around their neck. A broken hyoid bone in the neck is almost always caused by manual strangulation, whereas a blue discoloration around the mouth and nose indicates smothering. If there are no rope marks on the neck, no bruising and the hyoid bone is intact, then the neck is likely to have been deliberately compressed, blocking blood flow from the vagus nerve to the heart which would result in heart failure.

FIRE AND FLAME

Many a murderer has attempted to conceal their crime by setting fire to the scene and trusting that the flames will consume the evidence, but an experienced pathologist can uncover the true cause of death even from a charred corpse.

The classic clue to an accidental death by fire is the presence of soot in the lungs and carbon monoxide in the blood, which will turn it a cherry red colour. Soot is the result of smoke inhalation which leads to suffocation. Toxicology might also reveal cyanide in the blood which is created when synthetic materials such as ceiling tiles and certain types of paint react with flames.

If there is no soot in the lungs and no carbon monoxide in the blood the deceased is very likely to have died of burns which will have the characteristic inflamed edges created during the aborted healing process, known as a 'vital reaction' (proof that the person was alive when the injuries occurred). If none of these features is present and there is evidence of pre-burn bleeding then it suggests that the victim died of injuries prior to the fire (see 'The King's Cross Fire' page 186).

DROWNING

Drowning is a comparatively easier case to determine, although the corpse becomes bloated and subject to corruption after several days' immersion in water. But if the body is recovered within hours of drowning the characteristic signs should still be apparent during an autopsy. The lungs and stomach will be swollen and filled with water. There may also be blood in the stomach and airways indicating burst blood vessels as the deceased over-exerted themselves in their struggle to breathe. In cases of accidental drowning there may be indications of a heart attack brought on by shock or a vagal inhibition which can occur when water floods the back of the nose, or hypothermia caused by a fatal drop in the body's core temperature after immersion in cold water.

Even bath water and the water in chemically treated swimming pools will contain microscopic algae known as diatoms and, although seasonal fluctuations can reduce the concentration of diatoms, if those found in the ingested water do not match those in the water in which the body was found, death must have occurred elsewhere.

case file

The Exact Time of Death

When police entered the home of Illinois businessman David Hendricks on 8 November 1983 they found a scene of sickening slaughter. Hendricks' wife Susan and their three children had been brutally slain with blows from a butcher's knife and an axe which the killer had had the presence of mind to clean before he left. The walls and ceiling were running with blood and the mattresses were caked in splatter and brain tissue. So when the distraught father pulled into his driveway later that night having returned from a business trip, police prevented him from entering the house to spare him the grisly sight. They also told him as little as possible about the horrific injuries his loved ones had suffered at the hands of their deranged attacker. It was therefore highly suspicious when very shortly afterwards Hendricks recovered sufficiently to talk to reporters and describe the scene in detail as if he had been there when the murders were committed.

Questioned again at length, Hendricks appeared to have an airtight alibi. He had left home at midnight on Friday 4 November and driven through the night to Wisconsin to have meetings with potential customers first thing the next morning. Over the weekend he made repeated calls to his family and neighbours after failing to get through to his wife on the phone. None of them had seen Susan or the children since the night he had left home, but they were all confident that his fears were unfounded. Apparently not satisfied with their reassurances, he called the police and asked them to check on his family to put his mind at rest. The phone company's record of the calls placed him across the state line, confirming his story. In addition, microscopic analysis of his clothes and his car failed to find any incriminating traces of blood. Of course he would have had time to clean himself up and discard any bloodstained clothing, but even to cynical homicide officers such a scenario seemed too unlikely to be worth considering seriously.

SUSPICIONS AROUSED

However, Hendricks' willingness to speculate with reporters on who might have been responsible for butchering his family aroused the interest of detectives whose first impressions had been that the scene had been staged. A deranged maniac would have ransacked the house in his rage, but the Hendricks' home did not betray signs of wanton destruction, nor even of a burglary that had gone tragically wrong.

But what reason would an apparently devoutly religious and successful businessman have for murdering his own family? Hendricks appeared to have neither the motive nor the temperament for committing such a horrific act.

But, as investigators discovered, it was his new-found success that had created the urge to kill. As the profits from Hendricks' orthopaedic equipment company grew he began to acquire a taste for good living, sharp clothes and the company of beautiful women. He became estranged from his wife whom he was forbidden from divorcing by the laws of his Christian fundamentalist faith and this inner conflict precipitated a mental breakdown which led him to butcher his family and then calmly walk away as if someone else had done it. However, suspecting that he had done it and proving it in a court of law were two different things.

The case hinged on the victims' time of death, because if it could be proven that they were killed before midnight then detectives could discard the deranged intruder theory and place David Hendricks at the scene of the crime. At the autopsy the pathologist examined the stomach contents of the three children which contained half-digested pizza which they had eaten between 6.30 and 7.30pm. One would expect that the meal would have passed into the lower intestine after two hours but the fact that it hadn't travelled that far meant that they had

David Hendricks outside prison in 1990

been killed before 9.30, when their father was still at home. The best the defence could do at the trial was to argue that the children had been playing energetically after their meal and that exercise is known for slowing the digestive process, but the experts concurred that this would delay digestion by only an hour.

Whatever sympathy the jury might have had for David Hendricks evaporated when they were presented with the image of a callous father who calmly fed his children then slaughtered them so that he could be free to pursue other women. It is an image Hendricks will have to live with every day for the full term of his life sentences, all four of them.

Hendricks gets a kiss from his second wife Pat

The Mysterious Death of Robert Maxwell

The thorough investigation into the mysterious death of billionaire publisher Robert Maxwell was a model of modern forensic procedure. It also demonstrated that in the digital age a pathologist is expected to be much more than an anatomist. He or she must also be a forensic medical investigator with the restlessly inquiring mind and the dogged patience of a trained detective.

When the lifeless body of Robert Maxwell was fished out of the waters off Tenerife on 5 November 1991, rumours were rife that the 68-year-old publishing tycoon had committed suicide to avoid the shame of bankruptcy.

Obituary writers were forced to rapidly revise their rags-to-riches stories when it became known that the Serious Fraud Office were looking into serious irregularities in the Mirror Group pension funds. It seemed that £426 million had disappeared, together with an additional £100 million from the Mirror Group accounts, just days before the fateful voyage.

The alleged theft was not a paper crime but a human tragedy, as many ordinary hard-working people had placed their life savings and their trust in 'Uncle Bob's' supposedly iron-clad savings fund. The revelation of irregularities on such a massive scale would have meant more than financial ruin for the larger-than-life empire builder. It would have brought more shame than he could have lived with.

When it became known that a £55 million loan from the Swiss Bank Corporation was due for repayment on the day he died and that failure to honour the debt would have brought in the receivers, all the signs pointed to suicide. Maxwell appeared to have taken the easy way out. Or had he? It certainly looked that way until a startling suggestion was made by the Maxwell family lawyer which was echoed by the publisher's own daughter, Christine. They claimed that financial irregularities had nothing to do with her father's death. As far as they were concerned, Maxwell had been murdered.

CONSPIRACY THEORIES BEGIN

Ten days earlier Maxwell had been named as an unlikely Israeli secret agent in a controversial new book and now he had apparently been silenced to prevent his alleged involvement in illegal arms deals being made public. It seemed like a desperate attempt on behalf of the family to put up a smokescreen until several witnesses came forward to verify that Maxwell's 450 ton motor yacht, the *Lady Ghislaine*, had been shadowed for several days prior to his death by an unidentified vessel with no visible markings, name or flag. Furthermore, a swimmer had been seen in the water when the boats had been at anchor, which raised the possibility that Maxwell might have slipped quietly overboard to begin a new life while a lifeless look-a-like had taken his place in the water. Ridiculous though the suggestion seems, it was a fact that the initial Spanish autopsy had described the corpse as having an 'athletic build' whereas Maxwell was a grossly overweight 20 stone. Was it simply a mistranslation or had there been a substitution to save Maxwell and his Israeli spymasters embarrassment?

A former stewardess on the yacht had reported overhearing Maxwell planning to fake his own death and escape to South America just a few months earlier, but even if this was true it could have been an idle fantasy prompted by the likelihood of impending financial ruin. However, Christine Maxwell was deadly serious to the point of detailing how her father's murder had been effected. She claimed an air bubble had been injected into his bloodstream to induce an embolism which would have been diagnosed as death by natural causes – a favourite method of international hit men. When it became known that the Spanish pathologists had discovered a tiny perforation below one ear for which they could not account, the conspiracy theorists went into overdrive. The only chance of separating fact from fiction was to hold an autopsy for, as every criminalist knows, 'the evidence never lies'.

A preliminary autopsy had been carried out by the Spanish authorities which concluded that Maxwell had died of a heart attack before he hit the water, an assumption which the family vigorously disputed. It was evident that they were laying the groundwork to contest a £20 million insurance claim which would only pay out in the event of accidental death. Later it transpired that someone had anticipated the Spanish pathologist's findings. There was no evidence of a heart attack and no physical evidence to indicate that Maxwell had died of natural causes before falling into the sea. The Spanish pathologist reputedly asked the Maxwell family if he could bring in UK forensic experts to assist him, but on each occasion he was refused.

Had Robert Maxwell been planning to fake his own death?

Maxwell on his yacht, *Lady Ghislaine*

THE EXPERT PATHOLOGIST ARRIVES

In the event the insurance company organized their own autopsy and hired one of the world's leading forensic pathologists, Dr Iain West, and his wife Dr Vesna Djurovic to uncover the truth. But time was against them. According to Jewish law the deceased must be buried within a week and Maxwell was due for a full state funeral on the Mount of Olives in Jerusalem on Sunday 8 November. By the time the body had been flown to Israel and the autopsy team assembled it was already Saturday night.

Unfortunately both the body and the boat had been compromised as far as forensic evidence was concerned. The *Lady Ghislaine* had returned to sea the day after its owner's death without fingerprints, footprints or any trace evidence being secured. More crucially, the body had been contaminated by the overuse of neat embalming fluid and several organs were missing, although the Spanish judge had had the foresight to order tissue and toxicology tests as well as scrapings from underneath the fingernails to determine whether there had been evidence of a struggle. No such evidence was found.

They also had to contend with a number of false leads, such as the pool of dried blood inside the skull cavity, or vault, which is a classic sign of haemorrhage. But in this case it was explained by the fact that the Spanish pathologists had not drained the skull completely but had instead filled it with embalming fluid, leaving a residue of blood to dry at the back of the skull.

The first question the autopsy team had to settle was that of identity. The matter was settled swiftly and simply by comparing X-rays of the victim's jaw with his dental records. Britain's leading forensic odontologist, Mr Bernard Sims, identified several identical features including a uniquely shaped filling that proved conclusively that the body was that of Robert Maxwell.

THE SEQUENCE OF EVENTS

There was some dispute as to the time of death, which is a critical detail to resolve if there is a suspicion of foul play. At 4.55am on the morning of his death Maxwell had called the bridge to request that the air conditioning be turned down. That was the last anyone had heard from him. The alarm was eventually raised at 11am, when a call was put through that he didn't answer. The captain went down to investigate and discovered that the staterooms were locked from the outside, which was highly suspicious.

After a massive air and sea search Maxwell's naked body was

spotted at 5.46pm, face upwards and with his limbs outstretched. This in itself was unusual. Suicides do not usually drown themselves while naked and when they do they are invariably found face down and in the foetal position. If a body is found naked it suggests that drowning was the result of an accident. It was known that Maxwell slept naked and was in the habit of relieving himself over the edge of the boat during the night at a point where only a thin wire prevented him from falling into the sea. But at that point there was only a 30cm (12in) gap between the wire and the motor launches, which was too narrow for a man of Maxwell's bulk to fall through – and if he had fallen at that point he would have been sucked under the boat and cut up by the propellers.

Also, the sea was calm that morning and the stabilizers were engaged, so there was no reason to suppose that a sudden swell had tipped him over the side. He couldn't have fallen overboard anywhere else because there were guardrails running the full length of the yacht from prow to stern. He would have to have deliberately climbed over them, or been manhandled over the side.

Moreover, the crew of the search and rescue aircraft had scoured the area where the body was later found and had seen nothing, although it was possible that the body had floated to the surface just before it was sighted. Maxwell's obesity meant that his body could not be expected to behave in a typical fashion – that is, sinking below the surface for several days before resurfacing in a bad state of decomposition.

THE MYSTERY DEEPENS

The characteristic sign of death by drowning is water in the lungs and stomach and in the case of a drowning at sea the inrush of salt water raises the chloride level in the blood on the left side of the heart. There was surprisingly little salt water in Maxwell's lungs. One explanation is that he died from heart failure when he hit the cold water which would have prevented him from taking in any more water.

The absence of rigor mortis gave the pathology team further cause for concern, raising the possibility that the body could have been dumped shortly before it was sighted. If Maxwell had entered the water shortly after his request to turn down the air conditioning, he would have been in the water for 12 hours and rigor mortis should have been evident as it sets in more quickly in water than on dry land, although the temperature of the water is a factor. But then it occurred to Dr West that rigor mortis might have been dissipated when the body was hauled out of the water by the helicopter as movement of the limbs is enough to break up the condition. There is also the possibility that the rigor mortis had simply passed over some time earlier.

A pathologist has to be particularly thorough in an important case such as this one, and Dr West insisted on sending a sample of Maxwell's bone marrow back to England for analysis together with a sample of sea water from the spot where the body was found. The purpose was to see if there was evidence of diatoms, a microscopic plankton which one would expect to find in the lungs of someone who had drowned. They were not found in Maxwell's body, but neither were they detected in the sea water. The mystery was explained by the fact that the diatom population is extremely low in that region at that time of the year. Other clues would have to be found.

There were various bruises and abrasions on the body, some of which were caused by the Spanish manhandling the body during its recovery from the sea, but there was a suspicious looking bruise on the forehead which could not be explained. Had Maxwell hit his head on the side of the boat during a fall or a suicide attempt, or had he been pushed over board and struck his head as he fell?

The evidence was inconclusive because a bruise sustained during a struggle in the cabin would be identical to one sustained post mortem during a tumble overboard. But there were no restraint marks which are a typical sign of a struggle.

Internal examination offered a likely clue. The team found up to 95 per cent blockages in some of the coronary arteries and this, combined with Maxwell's behaviour that morning, indicated heart problems, though not necessarily a full-blown coronary. He had complained of nausea and of feeling hot and cold. There were traces of vomit in his respiratory tract and in his lungs and traces of seasickness pills in his system.

It was beginning to look likely that he had lost his balance while retching over the side and then suffered a fatal heart attack from the shock of the fall and the coldness of the water. There was evidence of heart and lung disease in the tissue samples but it was not sufficiently advanced to be the primary cause of death. Moreover, if Maxwell had suffered a heart attack, he would have dropped on to the deck and not tipped over the side.

Then, as the dawn was approaching over Tel Aviv, the pathology team made a significant discovery. After rolling the body on to its front they cut and folded the skin back to reveal extensive haemorrhaging and torn muscle fibres on the left shoulder as well as on the lower left side of the spine which also exhibited extensive bruising. This, coupled with bruises found on the right shoulder, on the right side of the neck and behind the right ear, indicated that Maxwell must have been clinging on to something such as a guard rail after having fallen overboard and banged the back of his head on the side of the boat as he twisted round. But his excessive weight would have torn the muscle, causing him such sharp pain that he would have let go of the rail and plunged into the water.

In his report to the insurance company Dr West concluded that there was no evidence of murder and that suicide was the most likely scenario. To Dr West the muscle tear indicated that Maxwell had fallen overboard accidentally perhaps while contemplating suicide and had instinctively grasped at the rail but then lost his grip through pain. If he had been attacked by an intruder and murdered, he would most likely have been knocked unconscious as he fell and then he would probably have been thrown cleanly overboard.

The fact that Maxwell went over at a point where there was a protective rail made an accident highly unlikely and suggested that he must have intended to go overboard, so his death must be assumed to be a suicide. The insurance company kept their £20 million payout and no doubt considered Dr West's fee and his expenses money well spent.

The family gathers for Robert Maxwell's funeral

Chapter 6
Forensic Anthropology

Not all murderers leave behind a fresh corpse that can be readily identified and examined for clues. Some dismember their victims in a desperate attempt to make identification impossible or bury the body where it will lie undiscovered for months or even years. Sometimes there is little more to go on than a fragment of bone. But no matter how decomposed a body might be when it is finally uncovered, or how little there is left to identify, the forensic anthropologist, with his expert knowledge of the human skeleton, has the skills to determine the manner of their death and lead investigators to the person or persons responsible.

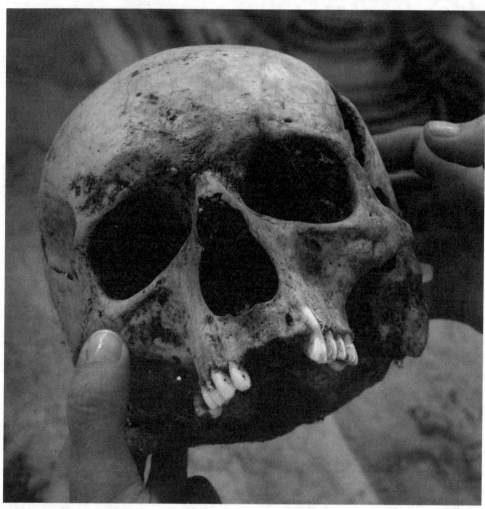

The skull has characteristics that vary between the sexes

IT'S ALL IN THE BONES

Even in these days of high-tech forensic science many killers still believe that if they can dismember, burn or severely degrade their victim's corpse they will render it unidentifiable and increase their chances of literally getting away with murder. But even skull fragments or a single bone can be enough to identify a body and determine the manner of death. No matter how badly decomposed, charred or fragmented a corpse may be, it is still possible for an experienced forensic anthropologist to determine the age, gender, physical build and ethnic origin from a few key features of the skull and skeleton.

Ethnicity can be determined by examining the shape of the skull. Caucasians have long, broad skulls with receding jawlines and comparatively flat cheekbones; the typical Asian skull is flatter, elongated and distinguished by the prominent cheekbones, oval eye sockets and the fact that the bridge of the nose is lower than that of a white person. In contrast, the shape of the African skull is narrow with wider nostrils and larger teeth.

The width of the pelvis and the shape of the sacrum (the fused vertebrae at the base of the spine) are the best indicators as to whether the victim was male or female, both being narrower in males. But the skull also has characteristic features which vary between the sexes. A bone at the back of the skull known as the occiput and a bone beneath the ear are both more pronounced in men, as is the ridge above the eye socket. In cases where only a few bone fragments are recovered it is still possible to determine gender from the thickness of the bone. Male bones tend to have larger ends to support their stronger muscles.

INFORMATION FROM THE SKELETON

By examining the size and density of specific bones a forensic anthropologist can determine the stage of skeletal development, which is a reliable indicator of age. The skeleton of a child is quite distinct from that of an adult not only in size and density, but also in the amount of cartilage at the joints linking the individual bones.

Conversely, if the skeleton shows signs of degeneration, then it is almost certainly the remains of an elderly individual.

If the skeleton can be reassembled the height and build of the person can easily be determined, otherwise individual bones can provide a clue to their stature and physique. The length of the femur (thigh bone), for example, is a reliable indicator of height. To determine a person's height from their thigh bone all the anthropologist has to do is multiply its length by three.

Further clues to the individual's identity can be found by examining the condition of the bones, which can betray their medical history, the means by which they met their death and even their occupation. Blows from a blunt instrument will shatter bones, producing tiny splintered shards,

A leg bone is washed after being collected from a mass grave

bullets will leave characteristic holes and sharp-edged weapons can chip and score the bone. Previous injuries such as fractures leave recognizable scars, while severe disability, chronic illness, arthritis and even occupational wear and tear can leave their mark on the skeleton, providing more clues.

SKULL SCULPTURE

When a corpse is discovered in an advanced state of decomposition and there are no clues to its identity, the only hope of putting a name to it is to reconstruct the face feature by feature, either with clay applied to the actual skull of the victim, or by generating a three-dimensional computer image. When investigators have an accurate likeness they can then circulate it in the hope that a friend or family member will finally be able to say who it was.

Unlike forensic artists, forensic sculptors do not have the benefit of a witness description, but instead are guided by the fact that although each human face is unique, variations in the shape of the skull determines our characteristics and these can be reconstructed using a system known as morphometrics. This technique, also known as the American method, identifies between 20 and 35 anatomical landmarks where the depth of tissue can be predicted with a high degree of accuracy. The only variations which the sculptor needs to be aware of are those relating to age, gender and ethnicity. They may even manage to get the hair style and colour correct if hairs were found on the body. But they have to use their imagination when it comes to the general facial shape as they cannot know if the subject was fat or lean unless the rest of the bones were also recovered, since their density can often give a clue as to someone's physical appearance.

Facial reconstruction was developed at the end of the 19th century to help anthropologists visualize the appearance of primitive man from fossil remains, but it wasn't applied to forensic detection until the 1930s. Data regarding tissue density had been acquired from anatomical specimens during dissection, but is now more easily and accurately obtained from living subjects using ultrasound.

SHAPING THE SKULL

If a complete skull is not available it can be reconstructed from fragments cemented together like a three-dimensional puzzle and then a cast can

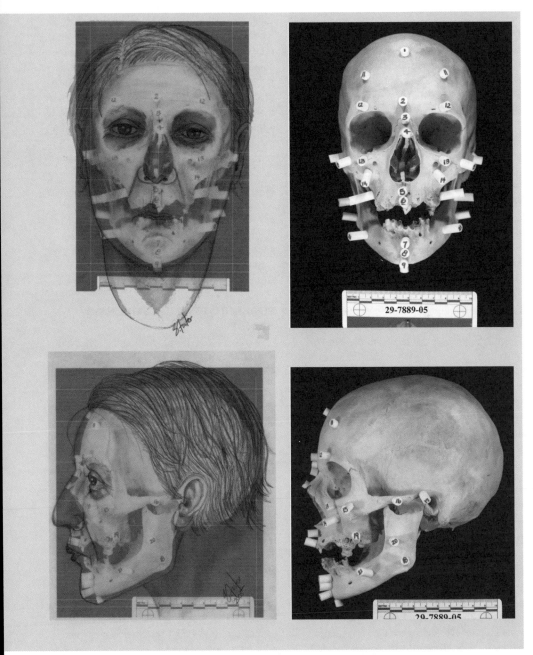

A forensic artist completes a likeness with information gleaned from the skull using the morphometric method

be made to provide the sculptor with a sturdy framework. Pegs of varying lengths are attached at the key points to indicate tissue depth and strips of clay of a suitable thickness are applied according to the height of the pegs. The moistened strips are then smoothed over so that the pegs are just below the surface and the clay is worked to shape the contours of the face.

Next, the features are formed with the proportions and placement conforming to certain anatomical principles such as the fact that the mouth corners usually align with the irises and that the nose is as broad as the space between the corners of the eyes. When the head is finished and glass eyes have been fixed in their sockets a plaster mould can be made, which is then painted in flesh tones and the mouth and eyebrows coloured to bring John or Jane Doe vividly back to life.

In contrast, the morphoscopic method, also known as the Russian method, assembles the face muscle by muscle according to the shape of the skull. Each muscle is formed in clay and then attached to build up the face before a thin 'skin' of wet clay is applied to blend them together.

Practitioners of the American method argue that their approach is more scientific and therefore more reliable, while proponents of the 'rival' system contend that their technique allows for atypical features which do not conform to regulation physiological formulas. Both methods have proven effective in identifying anonymous victims of violent crime, so the debate appears somewhat academic.

THE ART OF FACIAL RECONSTRUCTION

Computer-generated facial reconstructions are achieved using a similar method to forensic sculpturing except the modelling is done using a powerful PC program rather than a physical medium such as clay. After the skull has been scanned from every angle the data is compiled to produce a three-dimensional image on to which the 35 landmark pegs are positioned and fine-tuned by the programmer. Flesh is then applied using data obtained from scans of living subjects which recorded both the shape of their skull and their contours of their face. This ensures that the computer image will not be flat but will have all the textural features that make each human face unique. The CT (computer tomography) scan must then be 'warped' around the skull and adjusted to ensure a perfect fit in much the same way that a thin latex mask is applied to an actor's face.

A 'colour map' of a living person of the same race, age and gender is used as a tonal reference before eyes are sourced from a database which contains every likely combination of shape and colour. Finally, hair is digitally painted on but kept as straightforward as possible and shadows are added at the programmer's discretion to create a photographic lifelike image that will provide the best chance of recognition.

FORENSIC PROFILE: FORENSIC ARTIST

Forensic art involves more than simply sketching 'identikit' portraits of suspects or missing persons from witness descriptions. A forensic artist may also be called in when law-enforcement agencies require an up-to-date visual of a fugitive who has not been photographed for some time, or who may have changed their appearance. A skilled and imaginative artist may also be required to create post-mortem portraits to aid identification, or to re-create facial features when there is little more than a skull to work with. In such cases they will need to have studied the physiological changes which occur after death and be familiar with the craniofacial patterns associated with ageing.

Although there are dedicated software programs that can generate a suitably aged portrait, these still require a degree of artistic skill to create a realistic, workable likeness and many law-enforcement agencies feel that there is no comparison to a portrait sketched by a talented artist who captures the presence of a person and not just their physical appearance.

The greatest challenge for a forensic artist is to re-create a person they have never met from a badly decomposed corpse or a pile of bones. A certain amount of anatomical training will give them reliable guidelines as to the fullness of the cheeks, the shape of the nose and so on, but the 'art' in being a good forensic artist comes from being able to imagine someone from the clues given by their clothes, wristwatches and rings or the size of their bones and remnants of the muscle attachments.

BUILDING UP A PICTURE

When working on a composite portrait, to give an identikit sketch its official name, the artist must keep in mind that descriptions are highly subjective and their reliability is dependent upon many factors, including the duration of the incident, the distance from the suspect, the point of view, the available light, whether the subject was stationary or moving and at what speed, the time that has been allowed to lapse between the incident and interviewing the witness, and lastly the witnesses' eyesight and memory.

But even the most reliable eyewitness can have been unduly influenced by their emotional involvement in a violent incident. If they were upset they might elaborate or instinctively give a stereotypical description which may unconsciously express a prejudice they may have toward a certain race, class, age or type of individual.

There is some truth in the belief that if you ask five people to describe an individual they have just seen for a few seconds they will give you five different descriptions. The reason is that we tend to focus on a single feature – the eyes, an unusually prominent nose, a jutting jaw and so on. In contrast, a forensic artist focuses on the spatial relationship between the features. In this way they are able to capture the appearance of a suspect from a few unfocused frames recorded by a security camera.

However, forensic artists are sometimes forced to rely on instinct to a greater degree. Karen T.

Taylor, a forensic artist in Texas who has contributed to the capture of many predatory paedophiles and killers, 13 of whom ended up on death row, cites a case in which she had to provide the FBI with an update of Virgilio Paz Romero, who was then considered to be one of the world's most wanted men. Paz was a conspirator in the political assassination of the former Chilean ambassador to the United States, Orlando Letelier, in Washington, DC. With only poor-quality photocopies of photos of Paz to work from and the knowledge that he was an exuberant personality, Karen built up a picture of Paz as a self-satisfied larger-than-life character sporting a vibrant red shirt. The updated image was aired on *America's Most Wanted,* and when Paz was captured by US marshals three days later he was wearing a red shirt.

The computer can be used to build up a digital likeness

FORENSIC PROFILE: CRIMINAL PROFILER

It is not the job of the profiler to point a finger at a specific suspect, but to draw up a description of a personality type which the police can then use to single out the most likely suspect from a list of potential perpetrators.

The public perception of profiling, gleaned from popular American TV series such as *Profiler* and *Millennium*, is that it involves some form of near-psychic perception. In reality, it requires a mixture of psychological insight, an acute intuitive sense and a great deal of experience.

When a serious crime is committed the police have to decide within days if they will require the assistance of a profiler, since vital clues can be lost as the crime scene becomes contaminated by the weather if it is an exterior location, or disturbed by the investigating team.

Once assigned to the case a profiler will be sent a complete set of crime scene photographs, a detailed drawing of the crime scene showing the position of the body, plus a description of the location and surrounding area as well as some background concerning the lifestyle of the victim.

After studying the details of the crime and familiarizing themselves with the victim, the profiler can then focus on which direction the investigation should take. They will visit the location at the time the crime took place so that they can see for themselves what the perpetrator saw and perhaps pick out an important detail. For example, if it is a residential area and the crime took place when there was a lot of activity in the neighbourhood, it might suggest that the perpetrator was someone who would not be considered out of place, such as a delivery man or perhaps even one of the residents walking his dog.

Profiler, the US TV series: to be a criminal profiler you need intuition, psychological insight and experience

The Iron Age Murder Mystery

**You will not find the murder of Pete Marsh described in accounts
of infamous criminal cases nor in the files of Scotland Yard,
for Pete Marsh was not the victim's real name, but an appellation
given to a small heap of 2,000-year-old remains unearthed by
a mechanical peat excavator at Lindow Moss in Cheshire in
August 1984. Although both Lindow Man – to give him his official
title – and his killer were long since dead, this coldest of cold
cases was still of considerable historical interest to both
archaeologists and scientists around the world as it was
the oldest body ever found in Britain and it was in a remarkable
state of preservation.**

Incredibly, there were still strips of skin adhering to the bones and even
tufts of auburn hair, the remains of sideburns, a moustache and a
beard. The face was still largely intact, albeit hideously distorted,
although the lower half below the ribs had long since disintegrated.
In fact, it was such a significant find that the country's top forensic
anthropologists were called in to perform a belated autopsy and
determine the cause of death.

After a painstaking excavation the remains were transported to the
British Museum, where they were subjected to the intimate scrutiny of
modern technology. Terrestrial photogrammetry was employed for the
first time on a human body to sketch the contours of the corpse, while
his stomach contents were subjected to analysis by an electron spin
resonance spectroscopy and an endoscopy examined what was left of
his internal organs.

By the time the team wheeled in the X-ray equipment they had
concluded that prehistoric Pete had not died of natural causes. He had
been in his late twenties when he suffered a series of fatal injuries
including a dislocated neck and skull fractures. The team realized they
needed a second team of forensic pathologists to interpret the injuries
and so they approached Scotland Yard.

A SECOND AUTOPSY

The second autopsy was unusual for a number of reasons. Quite apart from the unique nature of the victim, it was a condition of the British Museum that none of the forensic team should be allowed to touch the body, which had been freeze-dried to preserve it as it was in such a fragile state. So they were forced to examine it using mirrors, magnifying equipment and X-rays.

Their findings surprised everyone and provided details of some pretty gruesome Celtic Iron Age customs that even the archaeological experts had been unaware of. This second autopsy revealed that what was originally thought to have been a necklace was in fact a ligature used to strangle the victim. The tissues of the neck had shrunk during decomposition rather than distending, which meant that the ligature had been pulled tight enough to choke the life out of him. The ligature mark was deeply indented and showed pressure abrasion suggestive of a garrotte. The position of the head wound, which had been sufficiently forceful to drive skull fragments into the brain, indicated that the victim must have been standing or kneeling with his back to his executioner.

The scalp lacerations were V-shaped, indicating two blows from a narrow-bladed, blunt-edged weapon such as an axe. Under a stereoscopic dissecting microscope the edges of the wounds revealed swelling that only occurs while the victim is still alive, so the blows were sufficient to render the victim unconscious without killing him. Fracture lines in the skull indicated a beating with a cudgel once the victim was lying senseless on the ground. An additional wound on the side of the neck was consistent with an attempt to sever the jugular vein with a sharp-edged weapon.

From all the information that had been collated it appeared that 'Pete Marsh' had been a ritual sacrifice, but this was not quite the end of the matter. It was only when the team received the results of the analysis of pollen, parasites and body tissues that the full story of his last hours could be told.

From this they were able to ascertain that Pete, or more properly the Lindow Man, was in fact a Druid prince called Lovernios, sacrificed to appease the gods after a bad harvest and the defeat of Boudicca in AD60. Incredibly, his stomach contents revealed the remains of an unleavened barley cake which meant that forensic experts were then able to date his death to the fire festival of Beltane (May Day).

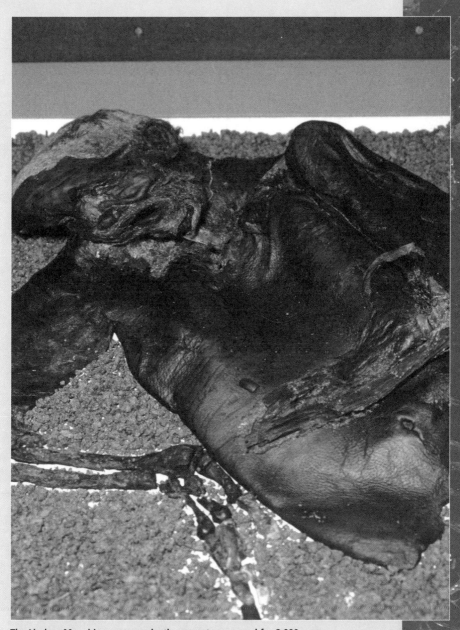

The Lindow Man: his gruesome death was not uncovered for 2,000 years

case file

The Mystery of the Romanovs

Perhaps the most unusual and intriguing case in which forensic techniques have been used to determine the identity of both the living and the dead is that of the last Russian Tsar and the woman who claimed to be his only surviving daughter, Anastasia.

In 1920, just two years after Tsar Nicholas II and his family mysteriously vanished in the confusion following the October Revolution, a young woman was fished out of a canal in Berlin, supposedly a failed suicide attempt. She appeared to be suffering from amnesia, but recalled just enough of her former life to claim that she was the Tsar's youngest daughter, the sole survivor of the Romanov dynasty. It was a claim she maintained until her death in 1984.

Eight years after her death a team of forensic scientists travelled to the former Soviet Union to identify a pile of charred bones that had been discovered in 1979 by a filmmaker, Gely Ryabov, who had been obsessed with solving the mystery of the missing Romanovs. Ryabov had been forced to keep his discovery a secret until the advent of *perestroika* for fear that the communist authorities would destroy the evidence, as the Tsar was still a potent symbol for many Russians and the state did not want to risk his remains rivalling those of Lenin as an object of pilgrimage – in this case for anti-communists.

The European forensic team were not concerned with the 'Anastasia' case. Their interest was in putting their combined skills to the ultimate test in solving one of the great mysteries of history. It had been assumed that the Tsar and his family had been summarily executed by their Bolshevik captors in 1918, but the bodies had never been recovered and the case of the woman who claimed to be Anastasia ensured that the question of their fate remained in the public consciousness. It was one of the great cold cases of the 20th century, until the American forensic anthropologist Dr William Maples and his team took a night flight to Siberia in 1992 to examine the skeletonized remains.

THE SKELETONS TELL THEIR TALE

The bones were to be identified by matching the measurements to those in the Romanovs' medical records and by superimposing X-rays of

The Czar, his wife and their young family aboard one of their yachts in 1907

the skulls on family photographs. But the team also had DNA from the recently disinterred body of Tsar Nicholas's brother for comparison and so were able to confirm that one of the Siberian skeletons was indeed that of the murdered Tsar.

The skull of Alexandra was readily identified by forensic odontologist Dr Lowell Levine, who had obtained her dental records from Germany, where the Tsarina had periodically returned to visit her family. Historians have argued that if the British royal family, to whom Alexandra was related, had offered a haven to the Romanovs the family might have escaped their fate. Certainly the royal connection proved critical nearly 80 years later when the forensic team managed to obtain blood and hair samples from Prince Philip, a direct descendant of Alexandra's grandmother, Queen Victoria, which proved a positive match when compared to DNA extracted from the remains.

Having identified which bones belonged to which victim, Dr Maples then meticulously rebuilt as much of the bodies as he could and then discovered that two of the victims were missing, Alexis and Anastasia.

It is believed that the remains of the two youngest children were left in a nearby mineshaft where all eleven members of the group had originally been taken to be burnt, but the Russians could provide no proof.

Fortunately the body of the Romanovs' physician was not completely skeletonized and provided two bullets from the First World War period, which helped to date the deaths to 1918.

But what of the woman who claimed to be Anastasia? Unfortunately, she had been cremated in 1984, but a tissue sample had been archived in a German hospital where she had once been a patient. DNA was extracted from this sample and compared to that donated by Prince Philip. There was no match.

The woman who claimed to be the Tsar's youngest daughter was, in fact, a Polish peasant by the name of Franzisca Schanzkowska who had been identified back in 1927 by a private investigator, but until the introduction of DNA testing his allegation could not be proved. Following the identification of the Romanov remains, one of her descendants provided a blood sample that proved a positive match to the DNA taken from the tissue sample obtained from the German hospital. Schanzkowska was an impostor, but it is a fact that the remains of the real Anastasia were never recovered.

Franzisca Schanzkowska who claimed to be Anastasia Romanov, the Czar's daughter

The MacIvor Case

When investigators first come upon a crime scene where there are multiple victims, they have to determine the nature of the crime with which they are dealing and identify which victim was the real target since it is possible that the other victims were innocent bystanders. Such was the problem facing FBI profiler Dayle Hinman in the case of the brutal murder of an attractive young couple, Missy and Michael MacIvor.

The MacIvors were discovered dead in their luxury home in the Florida Keys on an August morning in 1991. The initial suspicion was that it was a drug-related killing. Michael was an aircraft mechanic and pilot who had allegedly become mixed up with drug dealers, but thought himself 'bullet-proof', according to a friend. Four years earlier he had been arrested by customs for landing a plane with narcotic residue, but he had not been convicted. More recently he had bought himself a plane that had been impounded during a drug seizure and he was heavily in debt.

His body had been found on the living room floor, his eyes and ears covered with duct tape. His wife's naked body was discovered in the master bedroom at the foot of the bed. She too had been tortured and hog-tied (hands and feet trussed up behind her back in one binding) with a belt and a man's tie, then strangled with a cloth belt from a towelling robe. A ladder had been found propped up against a balcony outside the house and the phone wires had been cut, which indicated a degree of planning.

When FBI profiler Dayle Hinman saw the crime scene photographs she immediately discounted the drug connection. If it had been a drug hit, she reasoned, the killers would have brought their own restraints and weapons. Moreover, they would not have covered Michael's eyes and mouth if they had intended him to witness the torture of his wife or force him to give them information. Another clue lay in the fact that Missy's restraints had been tied and untied several times, indicating that she had been the object of the attack while Michael had been murdered merely because he had been in the way.

There were bruises on the back of his neck indicating that he had been struck repeatedly and once unconscious he was left alone.

A metal pole was found nearby that looked a likely murder weapon.

Missy had been repeatedly assaulted and strangled indicating that the killer was a sadistic psychopath who enjoyed dominating and tormenting his victims.

THE SEARCH FOR THE SUSPECT

As no other crime of a similar nature had been reported in the area in recent months, Hinman felt it safe to assume the murder was the killer's first and that he was following the usual pattern in having graduated from burglary to rape and finally to murder. On her recommendation detectives began combing the vicinity for likely suspects, since this type of criminal will begin his career in his own neighbourhood as he knows it well and will have his eye on escape routes should anything go wrong. This is what is known as the 'comfort zone'.

Within days a likely suspect was in their sights. Thomas Overton was a small-time cat burglar who fitted the profile. He specialized in breaking into houses where the owner was present. At the time he was working at a local gas station where Missy was a regular customer. This gave detectives a reason to question him but no right to arrest him. Until, that is, he was caught red-handed breaking into a house in the neighbourhood some months later.

Unfortunately, even a criminal caught in the act of committing a crime is not obliged to give a sample for DNA analysis, and with no hard physical evidence to connect Overton to the MacIvor murders there were no grounds for compelling him to submit to a swab under 'probable cause'.

But then the police had a break. While in custody Overton cut himself shaving and threw the bloody tissue away. It then became the property of the police and could be subjected to analysis. A search of the DNA database proved a positive match to the semen found at the crime scene. This was the kind of hard, irrefutable evidence that can crack a case, as there is a one-in-six-billion chance that it could belong to anyone other than the suspect. But it was not enough to prove beyond doubt that Overton had murdered the MacIvors, only that he had been in the house. The police needed to get Overton to deny that he had ever been in the house, then it would prove he was covering up the fact that he had been there on the night in question.

THE CASE IS CLOSED

The detectives devised a strategy to draw out a confession, based on the psychological profile Hinman had provided. They exploited his vanity by inviting him to the police station as an expert burglar to help clear up a series of unsolved break-ins. Overton was encouraged to believe that he might earn a shorter sentence if he cooperated and so he willingly looked through numerous photographs of houses, some of which he had burgled and some of which had been broken into by his associates. When the photograph of the MacIvor house was placed before him, he claimed he had never been there and so implicated himself in the murder. Had he admitted that he had broken in on the day of the murder a smart lawyer might have been able to argue that some unknown assailant had murdered the MacIvors after Overton had left. And as unlikely as that sounds, it might have sown sufficient doubt to get him a life sentence for sexual assault instead of a death sentence for premeditated first-degree homicide.

Florida Keys: the MacIvors were living here when they were brutually murdered

case file

Digital Identikit

For almost 16 years New Jersey detective Bernard Tracey was obsessed with finding elusive killer John List, who had murdered his 83-year-old mother, his wife and their three teenage children in December 1971 allegedly to spare them the indignity of his inevitable bankruptcy. It was initially assumed that List had subsequently taken his own life, but after his car was found at New York's JFK Airport and it was discovered that he had withdrawn $2,000 from his mother's account on the day of the killings, a coast-to-coast manhunt was launched in the hope of apprehending him. The search was later extended nationwide and eventually on to Europe and Africa in the belief that List's fluency in German might have enabled him to make a new life abroad.

But the trail ran dry and in desperation Detective Tracey turned to a newly developed forensic computer program which could replicate the effects of ageing. But first Tracey consulted Michigan profiler Dr Richard Walter, who created a psychological profile of the fugitive so that the effects of his lifestyle could be envisaged by the computer.

Dr Walter predicted that List's Lutheran religious beliefs would have prevented him from resorting to plastic surgery and that he would be inclined to a plain 'meat and potatoes' diet. This, together with his distaste for physical exercise, would have resulted in slack jowls and an appearance considerably older than his actual age.

After List's last known photograph was scanned into the computer the image was digitally manipulated to simulate the effects of ageing, poor diet and lack of exercise. A receding grey hair line and pale complexion were complemented by thick-rimmed spectacles which Dr Walter believed List's money-conscious conservative nature would encourage him to wear. Then the digital indentikit was broadcast on an episode of America's Most Wanted, prompting a flood of phone calls including one from a lady who named the man as her ex-neighbour, 'Bob Clark'. Mr Clark was duly questioned and, despite protestations to the contrary, his fingerprints proved beyond a reasonable doubt that he was indeed John List. Twenty years after he slaughtered his family then calmly relocated to Denver, Colorado, to start a new one, John List was sentenced to life imprisonment.

John List who murdered his family to escape debt

Odontology – Once Bitten

During 1993 the 'sunshine state' of Florida was making headlines for all the wrong reasons. It had become a stalking ground for opportunist thieves who considered tourists easy prey. Unfortunately, holidaymakers were not difficult to spot as rental car companies marked each vehicle with a company sticker and the criminals relied on the fact that out-of-state visitors would be unlikely to be willing to return to testify, especially if court proceedings could be deliberately and repeatedly delayed on technicalities dreamt up by a shrewd defence attorney.

Over the course of that summer local muggers had become increasingly audacious and vicious, attacking visitors in broad daylight, relying on shock tactics to traumatize their victims and render them less than reliable witnesses. But one gang chose the wrong victim. Despite the adverse publicity German TV producer Helga Luest had no fears about taking a vacation in Miami with her elderly mother. She had recently wrapped up a special report on the Florida crime wave in which she offered safety advice to would-be travellers so she was confident she could take care of herself.

The holiday was all that she had hoped it would be, but on the morning of their return flight Helga took a wrong turning en route to the airport and mother and daughter soon found themselves in an unfamiliar neighbourhood. While Helga tried to get her bearings, a car drove up, blocking her exit, and two black males leapt out. One shattered the driver's window with a single kick while his partner screamed threats to Helga's elderly mother in the passenger seat. Helga fought back bravely, forcing the pair to abandon the robbery and flee empty-handed, but not before they had inflicted severe injuries on their distraught victims. Helga sustained two cracked vertebrae, a serious head wound and a spiteful bite mark in her arm so deep that it had almost severed a muscle. Doctors later confirmed that had the attack continued it is almost certain Helga would have been left severely disabled.

A CLEVER DETECTIVE

Fortunately she recovered from her injuries and her case was assigned to Miami detective Laura Le Febvre, who had many years' experience investigating sexual assaults. Detective Le Febvre knew the forensic value of a fresh bite mark and had the foresight to arrange for it to be photographed under ultra-violet light which gives a three-dimensional image, making it easier to match to a dental impression taken from a suspect.

It was just as well that Le Febvre insisted on having the photograph taken as there were precious few other clues. The perpetrator who had left the bite mark lost his baseball cap in the struggle but it didn't help detectives because the hair samples inside didn't have a root and so there was no DNA to run through CODIS.

Just as the police began to despair of finding the perpetrators, Detective Le Febvre happened to visit the Miami-Dade Police department on an unrelated matter and overheard a conversation which put her on the trail of a prime suspect, factory worker Stanley Cornet. An officer was discussing the arrest of a suspect who had bitten him in an attempt to escape arrest. To make absolutely sure of a positive ID, Detective Le Febvre put Cornet's photo among 100 others, instead of the usual 10.

When Helga picked his picture out without hesitation Le Febvre organized a warrant for Cornet's dental impression. Knowing the game was up, Cornet protested violently and had to be restrained. Clenching his mouth tightly, he stubbornly refused to cooperate. It was then that forensic odontologist Dr Richard Souviron had an idea: he brought in a lethal-looking device that looked as if it might have played a part in the

Spanish Inquisition and placed it on the table before the belligerent suspect, the intimation being that he was ready to use it if Cornet continued to refuse to cooperate. In fact, the contraption was used

Helga Luest whose vacation in Miami with her elderly mother was cut short by a violent robbery

to prise open the mouths of cadavers during an autopsy. Dr Souviron had no intention of using it on the suspect, but the ruse worked and Dr Souviron secured an impression of Cornet's teeth which proved a perfect match to the bite mark on Helga Luest's arm.

Cornet was sentenced to life in prison, while Luest set up a victim support organization, www.witnessjustice.org, to offer advice to victims of violent crime.

Miami Beach: scene of many crimes in the 1990s

Last Will and Testament

Serious criminal cases are rarely resolved using just one type of forensic evidence. Frequently investigators will build a case on as many levels as possible to leave little room for error in case one type of evidence is ruled inadmissible for legal reasons or called into question by the defence's expert witnesses. In the case of the abduction and murder of 18-year-old Shari Faye Smith, her killer was caught and convicted using a combination of modern criminal profiling and good old-fashioned physical evidence.

Shari had been abducted in broad daylight and within sight of her home in Columbia, South Carolina, on 31 May 1985 as she stopped to collect post from the mailbox at the end of the driveway. Minutes later her father had found her car as she had left it with the engine running, the driver's door open and her purse on the passenger seat.

The police immediately organized the most extensive manhunt in South Carolina's history, but no trace of Shari was found. Later that day the Smith family received the first in a series of bizarre calls from the kidnapper, who disguised his voice with an electronic device. He proved that it was not a hoax by describing what Shari had been wearing under her clothes, but curiously he never mentioned the subject of a ransom. He appeared to enjoy tormenting the family, who still held out hope of finding Shari alive, and he promised that they would receive a letter the next morning.

The letter duly arrived. It was in Shari's handwriting and had been written on a sheet of lined legal paper headed 'Last Will and Testament'. It didn't give a clue as to her whereabouts, but it suggested she could still be alive. But in a subsequent call some days later her abductor said something which confirmed their worst fears. He said that Shari and he had become 'one soul' and he gave detailed instructions as to where they could find her body. It appeared that he had delayed giving them the location until he no longer had a use for her as a trophy and was certain that the body had decomposed sufficiently to degrade any useful forensic evidence. But there was also another reason – many killers keep the location of their victim's bodies a secret as they get a thrill from revisiting the site and reliving the murder.

A PROFILE IS COMPILED

The FBI Signal Analysis Unit concluded that the kidnapper's voice had been disguised using a Variable Speed Control Device, which suggested that he might have a background in electronics. This prompted the FBI to compile a profile which speculated that the man they were seeking would be in his late twenties or early thirties, single, overweight and unattractive to women. The fact that he indulged in cruel mind games, including calling the family reverse-charge on the day of Shari's funeral and describing in graphic detail how he had killed her, suggested that he was probably separated after an unsuccessful marriage and was likely to have a history of making obscene phone calls, all of which were to be proven correct. Two weeks later the same man abducted nine-year-old Debra May Helnick from outside her parents' mobile home in Richland County, 38km from the Smith residence. Then he phoned the Smiths and told them where the girl's body could be found.

It was about this time that the FBI had a break in the case. They subjected Shari's 'Last Will and Testament' letter to microscopic analysis using an ESTA machine, which detects the slightest impression in paper which would be invisible to the naked eye. It revealed a grocery list and a phone number which had been written on a sheet elsewhere in the pad from the one Shari had used. The phone number led detectives to the home of a middle-aged couple who had been out of the country during the period in which the murders had taken place. But they recognized the profile as an accurate description of their handyman, Larry Gene Bell, who they had allowed to live in their house during their absence.

Larry had aroused the couple's suspicion when he had picked them up from the airport and talked about nothing but the murders, and their suspicions were confirmed when agents played the couple a recording of Larry's final phone call to the Smith family in which he had not bothered to disguise his voice with the electronic device. His DNA was later recovered from the stamp he had licked before posting Shari's 'Last Will' and matched with a sample obtained on his arrest.

In 1996 Larry Gene Bell became the last person to die in the electric chair in the state of South Carolina.

Shari Faye's killer, Larry Gene Bell (left)

case file

The Railway Rapist

In real life, crime detection is rarely as simple as the fictional cases portrayed on TV. Fictional detectives invariably have a single suspect in their sights and have only to prove the case against them, while the dilemma facing real detectives is often to identify a guilty, faceless individual from among a million or more inhabitants of a major city. It is a process of painstaking elimination known as the 'needle in the haystack' method and it hasn't changed significantly in 200 years, only now we have computers to speed up the sifting process.

In 1986 the British police were working their way through a list of nearly 5,000 known sex offenders in the hope of catching a brutal serial killer known as the 'Railway Rapist', who had raped 27 women and murdered two more in London and Surrey, all near railway lines.

All the police knew for certain was that he was short, with a pockmarked face and fair hair and that, in the latest case, he had made crude attempts to destroy the evidence of rape by drowning his victim. They also knew that he had attempted to get rid of the evidence in the case of another of his victims by inserting paper into her vagina and setting it alight. Clearly he was a supremely callous and calculating individual.

After the second murder a man answering the vague description was seen running for the 6.07 train from East Horsley to London, prompting a frantic manual search through two million tickets, but no incriminating fingerprints were found.

By this time the police were getting desperate. They had a number of significant clues, including a length of string used to bind the victims' hands, and they had identified the attacker's blood group from semen stains. Analysis of the stains revealed the presence of an uncommon enzyme known as phosphoglucomutase which would eliminate a large number of suspects, but there was no time to interview every man on the list. The killer was likely to strike again at any moment and the police were stretched to breaking point trying to cover all the regional railway stations, which were unmanned by British Rail staff at weekends.

Railway Rapist John Duffy was jailed at the Old Bailey in London

WORKING AGAINST THE CLOCK

After Detective Chief Superintendent Vincent McFadden made the decision to pool the resources of all the various investigating teams in the Home Counties, the list was whittled down to a more manageable 2,000 suspects. Each was invited to give a blood sample, but one declined. His name was John Duffy, an ex-railway worker who fitted the description and had a record for rape and assault with a knife. But while the police were debating whether or not to risk arresting him without conclusive evidence he admitted himself to hospital suffering after what he claimed was a mugging, which had also conveniently robbed him of his memory. On his release he raped another woman, but the police still did not automatically link this to Duffy.

At this point in the investigation, McFadden turned to Dr David Canter, a professor of psychology at the University of Surrey, and requested a psychological profile in an attempt to identify the killer. Canter read the case reports and concluded that the so-called 'centre of gravity' connecting these crimes was a 5km (3 mile) area around the Finchley Road in north London and that the killer most likely lived in that neighbourhood. Among a further 16 points Dr Canter highlighted was the likelihood that he would be a semi-skilled worker who had experienced a volatile marriage and now had two close male friends. The data was duly fed into the computer and the name John Duffy was highlighted as a positive match.

A search of Duffy's home unearthed the unusual string used in the attacks and then one of the two friends admitted beating Duffy to give the appearance that he had been mugged so that he could claim to be suffering from amnesia. But the evidence which clinched the case was the discovery of 13 fibres on various items of Duffy's clothes which had come from the sheepskin coat of a victim he had tossed into the river and left to drown.

In the end, the DNA evidence was not decisive; Duffy was jailed for 30 years on the physical evidence and the testimony of three of his surviving victims, and with his conviction the era of this ever-elusive random sex murderer was ended. Since the days of Jack the Ripper sex killers had been notoriously difficult to catch and convict for the simple reason that their behaviour was impulsive and unpredictable. But a combination of computers, psychological profiling and genetic fingerprinting means that sex crimes are now as solvable as other crimes of violence.

Train travellers were asked if they had seen anything out of the ordinary

Chapter 7
Deadly Force

Criminals and terrorists used to believe that guns, bombs, arson attacks and even assaults using a vehicle afforded them a sense of anonymity. In recent years, however, forensic science has proven that nearly every weapon can be traced. Every gun leaves a distinctive marking on its bullets, explosive devices betray the handiwork of the bomb-maker, arsonists can be identified by their choice of accelerant and even mass-produced vehicles can be traced from a single fleck of paint. The weapons of choice may be becoming more sophisticated, but technology can tie criminals to the crime as effectively as if they had left their fingerprints at the scene.

BALLISTICS

Although it is a broad generalization, there is some truth in the belief that killers who choose a gun as their weapon do so because they unconsciously wish to demonstrate the total absence of emotional involvement that distance and the lack of physical contact affords them. But although guns are mass-manufactured, a firearm is not an impersonal or an anonymous weapon. Each weapon scores a unique series of signature markings on every bullet it fires as well as leaving gunpowder residue and other tell-tale trace evidence on the hands, face and clothes of the gunman.

However, while loading a weapon is likely to leave gun oil and microscopic traces of the soft metals used in ammunition on the gunman's hands, their presence proves only that the suspect handled a weapon. To prove that they fired it too, investigators look for soot deposits known as primer gunshot residue (P-GSR) on the trigger finger and will routinely swab both hands, the face and the suspect's clothes to establish a physical connection to the gun used in the shooting. P-GSR can be erased simply by washing the hands thoroughly with soap and water, but even the most thorough cleansing is likely to leave minute traces of its chemical components, barium, antimony and lead, which can be readily picked up using an atomic absorption spectrophotometer.

Semi-automatic pistols are the most common firearm used in gun crime today. Their self-loading mechanism means that up to 30 shots can be fired in rapid succession from a single magazine, avoiding the need for reloading. But such a sophisticated mechanism means that there are more components to put a signature on the bullet and its shell. Both the breech and the ejector mechanism mark the spent cartridge cases, while the firing pin and the rifling (a series of spiral grooves inside the barrel to increase the speed and accuracy of the bullet) score the bullet itself. Rifling grooves can be clockwise or anticlockwise and their spacing and width is arguably the single

most important feature in matching the bullet to the weapon from which it was fired. But equally important are the striations made on the shell casings by imperfections in the barrel. Under a comparison microscope two bullets can be compared side by side – one optically overlapping the other – to see if there is a positive match. Then the bullet or shell can be digitally scanned into the computer and a search run to see if the same weapon was used in other unsolved crimes. Even barrels rifled in the same factory differ microscopically as the tools alter with wear.

Ballistics experts need to be familiar with many types of firearms and be comfortable with using them on a daily basis as they will need to fire rifles, revolvers, semi-automatic pistols and even machine guns into water tanks, gel boxes and targets in order to recover sample bullets for comparison. But they may also be required to assemble weapons from parts that have been recovered from a crime scene by stripping down guns stored in the firearms cache at the lab. When a malfunctioning firearm is recovered or when only one part of a suspect's gun has been found it may be necessary to try to reconstruct the weapon from spare parts so that it can be test-fired and a comparison made with bullets and spent shell casings found at a crime scene.

BALLISTIC BREAKTHROUGHS

Prior to the invention in the mid-19th century of the revolver and the rifle, both of which leave distinctive markings on their bullets, the only way to secure a conviction solely on ballistic evidence was to prove that the calibre of the bullet recovered from the victim matched the calibre of the weapon owned by the suspect. This, however, was not sufficient proof of guilt if more than one suspect owned a weapon of the same calibre. Occasionally the police were lucky enough to be able to match the paper wad used to secure the bullet in a muzzle-loading pistol with scraps of the same paper found in the killer's possession. The murder of Edward Culshaw in Lancashire, England

Every gun scores a unique mark on each bullet it fires which means that they can be traced back to the original weapon

in 1794 was solved in this manner when police recovered a fragment of a street ballad from the fatal wound and were able to match it to a torn song sheet found in a suspect's pocket, making it the earliest recorded case solved by forensic ballistics.

A more sophisticated method was employed in 1835 by Bow Street Runner Henry Goddard, who unmasked a clumsy attempt by a butler to deceive his employer into believing that he had foiled an attempted burglary, presumably in the hope of receiving a reward. Instead the butler was summarily dismissed when Goddard proved that the bullet supposedly fired into the headboard of the butler's bed by the intruders had, in fact, been fired from the butler's own gun.

Goddard's suspicions had been aroused when he noticed that the jemmy marks on the butler's door and on the door frame were not aligned as they would have been if someone had tried to prise open a locked door with a crowbar. He continued his investigation and noticed the same discrepancy on the cupboard in which the 'stolen' silverware was kept. When Goddard compared the bullet lodged in the headboard with those in the butler's gun he saw that they were suspiciously similar. He then examined the mould used by the butler to cast his bullets and observed that both the 'burglar's bullet' and the

butler's home-made bullet had a small dimple corresponding to a hole in the mould.

TWENTIETH-CENTURY BALLISTICS

It was not until 1912 that ballistics was officially recognized as being as powerful a weapon against crime as fingerprinting. At the Congress of Legal Medicine in Paris that year, legal expert Professor Victor Balthazard entertained his colleagues with details of a recent case on which he had been consulted by the French police.

A suspect named Houssard was being held on suspicion of shooting a man named Guillotin because his gun matched the calibre of the bullets found in the victim, but prosecutors were reluctant to proceed because the bullets had fragmented inside the body. Professor Balthazard pieced together the bullets and then compared the markings of those recovered from the corpse with one fired in the laboratory using photographic enlargements. He identified 85 distinctive characteristics including grooves or striations created by the rifling inside the barrel as well as markings made on the cartridge case by the firing pin and other parts of the gun. Houssard was convicted and Balthazard earned himself a place in forensic history as the father of ballistic science.

An Australian forensic team investigate the scene of the bomb at Bali in 2002

BOMB SCENE INVESTIGATIONS

The most demanding aspect of a bomb scene investigation is not tracing the bombers but identifying and collecting fragments of the bomb, which will have been scattered over a large area and buried among tons of debris. Once the components have been collected and the device reassembled, it is a comparatively simple job to identify the type of explosive used and trace the individual responsible as almost every device carries the signature of the bomb-maker.

After every incident involving explosives the investigative team must follow a rigid protocol to ensure they collect every possible surviving trace of the device and avoid contamination under the most difficult conditions.

The first stage is to establish the centre of the blast and cordon off an area that can be divided into grid squares like a chess board. This enables investigators and later the legal team to pinpoint where specific items were found after the blast. An initial walk-through to collect the larger bomb fragments will be followed by a more thorough fingertip search, concentrating on those areas where shattered fragments of the device had been found on the first pass.

Then the debris is swept into the centre of each square using sterilized brushes and each pile is sifted in the search for wires, batteries, timing devices, nails, ball bearings and twisted fragments of the casing. But even the most thorough searches can sometimes overlook vital clues, especially if there is a large amount of material scattered over a very wide area, as was the case in the Lockerbie bombing of 1988 (see page 185).

Once the area is cleared and any structural damage to the building has been temporarily secured, forensic experts can move in to search for

residual traces in the hope of identifying the type of explosive used in the attack. Often the choice of explosive will point to a possible perpetrator or at least suggest a fruitful avenue of investigation. Semtex was at one time the preferred explosive of the IRA, fertilizer has been a popular ingredient with home-grown terror groups such as the Oklahoma City bombers of 1995, while pipe bombs are the most common form of home-made bomb created by lone murderers (see 'Mail Order Murder' page 182).

During their search forensic explosive experts will use vapour-analyzers, which act like robot sniffer dogs, and apply chemical reagents to suspicious stains which produce a positive reaction when in contact with specified explosives in much

Securing the area to prevent contamination after an explosion

the same way that luminol does when it comes into contact with blood.

In the lab the recovered debris is examined in greater detail to determine if it is part of the bomb or otherwise relevant to the investigation. If it is a significant find then it is subjected to microscopic analysis and the customary toxicology tests. Any recovered residue which appears to be latent explosive or is suspected of having been in contact with either explosive or the bombers will be dissolved in a solution of acetone and water so that it can be subjected to further tests.

ARSON

The destructive power of fire has been used by criminals desperate to eliminate the evidence of their crimes, be they murder or insurance fraud, as well as by arsonists who often report experiencing a vicarious thrill from watching

Handle with care: plastic explosive Semtex is difficult to detect as it has no smell

flames consume a building they have set alight.

Arsonists are notoriously difficult to trace, as the nature of fire means that most physical evidence will have been consumed by the flames. However, a celebrated Japanese detective, Asaka Fukada, was able to predict a large number of arson attacks in the 1980s simply by studying the weather reports. His theory was that there is a certain type of fire-starter who sets buildings ablaze in order to relieve breathing difficulties caused by low atmospheric pressure. The image of the rising flames evidently alleviated the sense of suffocation. Others would act out of pure maliciousness or spite, such as disgruntled employees, spurned lovers and even a vengeful schoolboy who had failed an exam. These Inspector Fukada would 'out' not by accusing them of the crime but by appealing to their ego. Catching them in an off-guard moment, he would ask them casually how long the image of the fire had remained in their minds to which they would impulsively answer with evident pride, their eyes glazing over as they recollected the scene.

Modern CSIs take a more scientific approach but often achieve equal success by examining specific features that even the most intense conflagration cannot erase.

Accidental fires invariably have one point of origin, such as a poorly wired electrical point or a spot where an inflammable substance was inadvertently set alight. In contrast, arsonists typically set a number of fires to ensure that the blaze will spread. Investigators will begin at the lowest level of the building where fire damage is evident in the knowledge that fire spreads upwards so there is less likelihood of finding an ignition point on the higher levels. Clues can be found in the smoke patterns and charring which discolour surviving walls, floors and ceilings.

To the trained eye a burnt building can be read in a similar way to a dead body – its wounds betray the manner of its destruction. Spalling (the sequence and degree of damage to structural surfaces) can lead investigators to the source of the blaze, as can the specific type of damage to the furniture and fittings.

CHECKING ALL THE EVIDENCE

Having found the primary source of the blaze there is then a choice of equipment available for identifying the accelerant, which could be anything from a home-made petrol bomb to a sophisticated explosive device set off by a timer or signal from a mobile phone. Fortunately, investigators are now armed with devices such as hydrocarbon vapour detectors which sample the surrounding air and detect the presence of a chemical accelerant which will remain even after the most intense fire.

But an experienced investigator will rarely have to rely on high-tech equipment. Inflammable liquids such as paint thinner and solvents leave pungent odours that linger in the air long after the flames have been extinguished, as well as burn patterns and stains on flooring where they pooled when ignited.

In addition to combing the immediate area for footprints, tyre tracks and signs of forced entry, the investigation team will also closely examine alarms and sprinkler systems to see if they have been disabled. Whether it is a private residence, a public building or a place of business, detectives will question the owners as a matter of routine to determine if there might be someone they suspect of having a grievance against them. Anyone suspected of having a motive for arson would be interviewed and their clothing and footwear examined for any traces of accelerant or other trace evidence to link them to the scene.

Suspect vehicles are blown up in controlled explosions, particularly when a terrorist attack is threatened

case file

A Fatal Falling Out

Computer-generated reconstructions are becoming a familiar feature of murder trials in the United States, but there is increasing concern that juries are accepting them as factual representations of what happened, rather than as just one possible scenario. The dangers of accepting computer-generated reconstructions as evidence was highlighted in 1991 at the trial of Californian pornographer James Mitchell.

Forty-year-old James was on trial for the murder of his younger brother Artie. There was no denying the fact that James had killed Artie, for the five shots that had left the hard-drinking, drug-taking strip-club owner lifeless in the bedroom of his San Francisco home had been caught on tape by a 911 operator.

The question was, had James planned the shooting, or was it committed in the heat of the moment? The distinction was critical as premeditated murder carried a mandatory life sentence in the state, whereas manslaughter would put him away for just five or six years. The pair were known to have had heated arguments that frequently resulted in an exchange of blows, but they had always managed to bury their differences before either had suffered a serious injury. But on the 27 February 1991 it was different and their partnership was terminated, permanently.

At 10.15pm that night police arrived at the scene to find James pacing up and down outside the house in an excitable state, brandishing a .22 rifle and sporting a .38 Smith and Wesson revolver in a shoulder holster. Once he had been disarmed they went inside, where they discovered Artie's body. He had been shot in the stomach, the right arm and in the right eye. Eight spent .22 shell casings were found nearby.

CRUCIAL DETAILS

At the trial the prosecution argued that the long space between shots, which could be clearly heard on the 911 tape, clearly demonstrated intent. Had it been a spontaneous shooting the shots would have been fired in quick succession.

Based on spectrograms of the shots, forensic acoustics expert Dr Harry Hollien was able to identify where each shot on the tape occurred. From this the prosecution were able to create a computer-generated video animation of the murder in which a figure representing Artie was shown being pursued by another – his attacker.

In court the film was accompanied by a commentary from Arizona criminalist Lucian Haag, who explained that the sequence of events had been determined by tracing the trajectory of the bullets to the impact points and reproducing any deflections in the crime lab. Haag had even gone to the trouble of buying a door like the one in the victim's house and shooting at it so that he could measure the angle of deflection under controlled conditions.

Such thoroughness impressed the jury, but the defence successfully argued that, with so many bullets, there were thousands of possible variations and that the video animation was only one scenario, albeit the most likely. The judge ruled that the video was to be treated as speculative, not definitive. It was not the job of the crime scene investigators to imagine the scene, but to present the facts and interpret the science.

Without a material witness to give evidence as to James Mitchell's state of mind at the time of the shooting and testimony as to the sequence of events that led up to the fatal shooting, the jury could not be expected to find him guilty of first-degree murder. Consequently James was acquitted on the murder charge but found guilty of manslaughter and sentenced to six years in jail.

Brotherly love: James and Artie Mitchell together in happier times

case file

The Libyan Embassy Shooting

Just hours after WPC Yvonne Fletcher was gunned down outside the Libyan Embassy in St James's Square, London on 17 April 1984, wild rumours were circulating in the media that threatened to ignite an already volatile situation in the Middle East. Some were of the opinion that she had been deliberately targeted by Israeli agents stationed on the roof of the embassy in an effort to spark a war between Britain and Libya which might have served Israel's interests. Others blamed militants among the anti-Gaddafi faction who had been protesting in front of the embassy when the shooting took place. It was therefore a matter of great urgency to discover the true identity of the gunmen if a potential conflict in the Middle East was to be avoided and the killers brought to justice.

Britain's leading forensic pathologist, Dr Iain West, performed a post-mortem on WPC Fletcher within hours of the shooting, during which he was surprised to discover that one single 9mm sub-machine-gun bullet had passed through her body, creating four distinct wounds in her back, abdomen and left arm. Suspecting that these entry and exit wounds were to be crucial in determining the trajectory of the fatal bullet and the location of the gunman, Dr West had them photographed. He then travelled to the scene while the siege was still in progress and stood where WPC Fletcher had stood, seemingly oblivious to the danger still posed by the gunmen inside the building. There were several witnesses among the protestors, police and bystanders who were willing to testify that they saw two gunmen firing from the first-floor window of the embassy, but the situation was so politically sensitive that the police needed irrefutable forensic evidence to corroborate their statements.

From the post-mortem photographs, Dr West was certain of the angle at which the bullet entered the victim's body and he knew from TV footage of the incident exactly where WPC Fletcher had been standing. She had had her back to the building and her arms were folded across her chest, which accounted for the multiple wounds as

Police attend to WPC Yvonne Fletcher moments after she was shot

the bullet entered her back, exited her abdomen and perforated her elbow.

Back at the laboratory, Dr West used an inclinometer to calculate a maximum angle and concluded that the bullet could not have come from the roof or from street level but must have come from the first or second floor of the Libyan Embassy.

THE EVIDENCE IS CLEAR

Despite this compelling evidence, the perpetrator was never brought before a British court to answer to the murder of WPC Fletcher. Desperate to resolve the stalemate in central London, Britain broke off diplomatic relations with Libya and expelled all of its diplomats, which meant that all 30 inhabitants of the embassy walked free from the besieged building, despite the fact that only 22 had full diplomatic status.

In the wake of the siege the police found discharge residues and other incriminating evidence of gunfire having come from a first-floor window,

as well as a cache of arms and ammunition including a weapon
that had been used to assassinate a Libyan journalist in Regent's Park
four years earlier.

At the inquest Dr West testified that WPC Fletcher had been so
severely wounded that no one could have saved her. The bullet had
entered her back at a 60-degree angle, passed through her liver, crashed
into her spine, sliced through the pancreas, re-entered the liver and
ruptured the main vein in her abdomen. There were nine other victims
at the scene treated for gunshot wounds, all of whom recovered.

Today a plaque marks the spot where WPC Fletcher died and
residents ensure that there are always fresh flowers beside it.

Armed police move in to surround the besieged Libyan Embassy

Hit and Run

Detectives usually have difficulty persuading the guilty to confess to their crimes, but in the case of the murder of 17-year-old Rosemary Anderson they had two conflicting confessions from two different suspects to choose from! How could they be sure they had charged the guilty man? It took 40 years and the use of a new forensic science to uncover the truth behind a serious miscarriage of justice and reveal the true identity of a hit-and-run killer.

On the evening of 9 February 1963, John Button invited his girlfriend, Rosemary Anderson, to his parents' house in Perth, South Australia, to celebrate his 19th birthday. During the evening they quarrelled and Rosemary stormed out, determined to walk home alone. John followed her in his car, a French Simca, talking to her as she walked along the dark, otherwise deserted roadside. But she was in a foul temper and refused his offer of a lift home, so he stopped and watched dejectedly as she disappeared round the next corner. Anxious not to leave her in this mood he decided to catch up with her, but when he did so he made a shocking discovery. Rosemary was lying face down at the side of the road, bruised and bleeding, the victim of a hit-and-run driver. In desperation John carried her limp body into his car and rushed to the hospital, but there was little the doctors could do. Rosemary died shortly after being admitted and John was charged with manslaughter.

The case hinged on the fact that there was damage to the front of the Simca and droplets of blood on the front bumper. John protested his innocence, but to no avail and after several hours of intense interrogation, during which he later claimed he had been beaten by the police, he confessed. Within hours he recanted, saying that he had only admitted guilt in an effort to end the interrogation and stave off another beating. In his defence John claimed that the damage to the car had been incurred weeks earlier and that the blood on the bumper resulted when he brushed past it when carrying Rosemary to the car. But the confession and the forensic evidence was sufficient to convict him. John was condemned to serve ten years' hard labour in Australia's notorious Fremantle Prison.

Seven months later, John thought his luck had turned when a prisoner informed him that a new inmate was boasting that he had intentionally killed a young girl for the fun of it in John's neighbourhood on the night in question. The driver was Eric Edgar Cooke, a psychopath who had been sentenced to death for a series of brutal murders. The police took Cooke to identify where he had run Rosemary down, but he pointed out the wrong place and so John's appeal was turned down. Cooke again confessed to Rosemary's murder on the morning of his execution, but it was not sufficient to free John Button, who was eventually released after five years in 1968 for good behaviour.

FREEDOM IS NOT ENOUGH

Free, but unable to live with the stigma of being labelled a convicted killer, John determined to clear his name. He found an unlikely ally in Estelle Blackburn, a female journalist who had been dating his brother. She was able to access files that had been closed to John and to interview people who would not talk to him about the case.

Estelle discovered that Cooke had confessed to six hit-and-run murders, but that this information had not been introduced at John's appeal. Convinced that John was innocent, Estelle enlisted the help of W. R. 'Rusty' Haight, an expert in the new forensic science of Pedestrian Crash Reconstruction, which Rusty liked to describe as 'common sense mixed with basic physics'.

Using a properly weighted and articulated bio-medical dummy suspended from a fishing line, which broke on impact, and a lightweight French Simca identical to John's car, Haight proved that the damage to the car was inconsistent with the injuries sustained by the victim. Rosemary had been hit at 48km/h (30mph), which leaves distinctive markings on the vehicle as the body folds around the front of the car with the head impacting on the bonnet to leave a noticeable dent. John's car did not have this damage when the police impounded it. Furthermore, Haight managed to obtain a 1963 Holden which was the car Cooke had driven when he claimed to have killed the six women. When the dummy was hit by the Holden it landed on its back in the position John claimed to have found Rosemary in, whereas when the Simca hit it the dummy landed on its face.

But one last question needed to be answered before the new evidence could be admitted in an appeal. Cooke's car had a plastic visor to shield the driver from glare and the police had always maintained that if Cooke had killed Rosemary the visor would have been damaged. But Haight was able to demonstrate that the flexibility of the plastic visor meant that it snapped back into shape after the impact.

Armed with this compelling evidence and Estelle Blackburn's best-selling book on the case, Button's lawyers were able to argue successfully that the original prosecution case was fatally flawed. It was only in 2000 that John Button was finally exonerated of the manslaughter of Rosemary Anderson having, in his words, been 'imprisoned by the injustice of the whole affair' for the previous 37 years.

After 37 years John Button was finally exonerated of his girlfriend's murder

case file

JFK and the Magic Bullet

Even those who have no patience with convoluted conspiracy theories must surely question the official government version of the John F. Kennedy assassination as presented by the Warren Commission, which concluded that a lone marksman was responsible for shooting the president and was then himself conveniently killed before he could be questioned in open court. Quite apart from the numerous inconsistencies, accusations of evidence-tampering and mysterious deaths of key witnesses, the forensic evidence alone challenges the idea that a single sniper killed President Kennedy in Dallas on that fateful November afternoon in 1963.

If the assassination was indeed orchestrated by disaffected elements within the administration and the armed forces, as has been alleged, those responsible covered their tracks extremely well, but they could not have foreseen that the fatal moment would be captured on film by amateur home movie buff Abraham Zapruder.

Despite several attempts to suppress the controversial footage, those images could not be airbrushed out of history like the numerous witnesses who swore to hearing shots and seeing puffs of gunsmoke coming from a location other than the Dallas Book Depository where the lone gunman, Lee Harvey Oswald, is generally supposed to have fired three uncannily accurate shots in quick succession from a faulty bolt-action rifle, a feat even trained snipers failed to copy in subsequent tests.

The Zapruder footage establishes a timeframe of 5.6 seconds from the first shot, when Kennedy is clearly seen to flinch, as he instinctively reacts to the bullet whizzing past his ear, to the last in the frame which quite clearly shows the front right side of the president's head being smashed by a bullet.

The bullet obviously could not have come from the direction of the Book Depository which the motorcade had just passed. And this is when the myth of the 'magic bullet' was born. One of the most famous scenes in Oliver Stone's film *JFK* is the monologue on the subject of the magic bullet.

A model reconstruction to try to determine the path of the gunfire that killed JFK

UNBELIEVABLE FACTS

If there were only three shots, as the Commission contends, then the first was the one which made Kennedy instinctively react and Senator Connally turn round in the front passenger seat to see what had startled the president. This first bullet appears to have ricocheted and a fragment of it, or piece of shrapnel, then struck bystander James Teague, who was standing by the underpass in front of the motorcade. If the third bullet caused the fatal head wound, then that leaves only one bullet responsible for the seven separate wounds in Kennedy and Connally. According to the Commission this 'magic bullet' entered the president's back at an angle of 17 degrees and was deflected upward and out through the president's neck, then suspended for 1.6 seconds after which it turned right and then left and entered the Senator's right armpit. It then headed downwards at an angle of 27 degrees, shattering Connally's fifth rib, and exited from the right side of his chest. We are then asked to believe that the bullet made a right turn and shattered Connolly's radius bone in his right wrist, after which it made a U-turn and buried itself in the Senator's left thigh.

Incredulity is stretched beyond breaking point by the assertion that this miraculous projectile then dropped out of the wound unnoticed and was later discovered in pristine condition on a stretcher at Parkland Hospital, where it proved a perfect match for Oswald's weapon. The Army wound ballistics experts at Edward Arsenal later fired identical rounds for comparison and all were severely distorted after striking just one bone in a cadaver.

Any forensic pathologist would know that the only possible explanation for the number of wounds and their angle of entry is that there were four shots, not three, and that would require at least two marksmen, maybe even a third. A triangulation of fire is standard set-up for a moving target in US 'black operation' assassinations. It establishes a killing zone that reduces the risk of the target escaping alive and is indicative of a CIA or military involvement. A ballistics expert who studied the location could see that a single assassin would have had a perfectly clear shot from the rear of the Book Depository as the motorcade passed slowly towards him along Huston and possibly even time for a second shot, whereas the view Oswald is said to have had of the president's car as it turned into Elm Street at the rear of the Depository was obscured by an enormous tree which retains all its foliage in autumn. Clearly someone in the conspiracy did not do their homework and reckoned without the tenacity of those who refused to take the official version at face value.

ANOMALIES AT THE AUTOPSY

At Parkland Hospital, Dallas, where the preliminary autopsy was carried out, no fewer than 26 medical personnel were witness to the fact that the back of the president's head had been blown away in a manner which could only have been caused by a shot entering the right side of the head. One of the attending physicians, Dr Peters, later testified that the wound was 7cm (2¾in) in diameter and that 'a considerable portion of the brain was missing'. Another observed that as much as a fifth or even a quarter of the back of the head had been blasted out and that a large fragment of skull remained attached to a flap of skin, also indicative of an exit wound.

Incredibly, the pathologist in attendance at the preliminary examination was asked to concentrate exclusively on the head wound and not to dissect the neck, which would have revealed the presence of a second bullet wound. Significantly, all of the civilian doctors who were present regarded the hole in the throat as an entry wound, but it was disregarded by the chief pathologist, Commander Humes, who, under instructions from the military observers, abruptly wound up the examination, to the consternation of the resident physicians. Humes is said to have later burned his autopsy notes.

The body was then transferred to a military base where it was examined by service physicians who would not have been free to publish their findings and who were under orders to prepare a report for the eyes of designated officers only. More revealing and disturbing is the fact that later the same day, President Lyndon B. Johnson ordered the immediate cleaning and repair of the presidential limousine, thus destroying crucial fragments of physical evidence including the bullet holes from which the angles of trajectory could have been calculated.

And many years later, when conspiracy-obsessed New Orleans DA Jim Garrison obtained a court order in order that he could examine the president's remains in the National Archive to determine the direction of the bullets, he was told by officials that the president's brain had been lost!

The presidential motorcade moments before the fatal shooting

case file

Mail Order Murder

When a home-made pipe bomb killed 17-year-old Chris Marquis in his home in Fair Haven, Vermont, detectives had little hope of catching the killer and that was because the lethal ingredients were common household items that could be purchased anywhere in the United States.

Neighbours often joked that Chris and his mother lived in the safest house in town – a bungalow right next door to the local police station. But one morning in March 1998 violent death came to Fair Haven in an innocuous-looking package. Christopher's mother suspected nothing as she carried the parcel to her son, although she didn't recognize the name of the sender or the return address. Chris ran a small CB radio sales and repair business from his bedroom and this looked as if it might be something that he had ordered from a supplier. But Chris didn't recognize the sender either. He opened it anyway and the next moment there was a tremendous explosion which tore a hole in Chris's leg and left his mother with serious injuries. Chris later bled to death in hospital, leaving his mother distraught and wondering who could have wanted her son dead and why.

Detectives soon had an answer to both questions. On Chris's computer, investigators found emails from angry customers claiming that Chris had cheated them by advertising an expensive radio over the internet and then sending a cheaper model in its place once he had cashed their cheques and pocketed the difference.

Suddenly they had several hundred suspects. But could any of them really have been so angry that they would take revenge by killing a 17-year-old that they had almost certainly never met?

While detectives trawled through the list of Chris's customers, forensic experts combed the bungalow looking for physical evidence that could give a clue as to the identity of the perpetrator. They found

The mother of bomb victim Chris Marquis with a photo of her son

Styrofoam packaging material and pieces of pipe, wire, grains of smokeless gunpowder and tiny hex nuts – all ingredients of a home-made pipe bomb, but nothing that pointed to a specific individual. The return name and address on the package proved to be fictitious and none of Chris's outraged customers lived in Mansfield, Ohio, where the package had been posted.

A LUCKY BREAK

But then they had a break. The story had made the national news and someone had phoned in with information. This anonymous source had recently been in a bar where he had overheard a long-distance truck driver complaining that he had been ripped off by a mail-order CB radio repair service in Vermont and was planning to go down there and teach the guy a lesson. The truck driver's name was Christopher Dean.

The detectives went to Dean's house in Indiana, where they found hex nuts of the type and size used in the bomb, lengths of wire and even a plastic funnel with grains of what proved to be smokeless gunpowder residue. But again, these did not amount to conclusive proof.

To find out if the hex nuts in Dean's house were the same as those found at the crime scene, forensic scientists took scrapings of both samples and placed them in a neutral solution before putting them in a plasma atomic emission spectroscope which vapourized the samples at an extremely high temperature. Different compounds such as zinc and copper vapourize at different speeds, revealing the chemical make-up of any metallic object, and computer analysis of the test results revealed that both sets of hex nuts had exactly the same chemical make-up. The residue of gunpowder found in the funnel was then analyzed by a scanning electron microscope which uses X-rays to identify the components of a given substance

Crude pipe bombs, as seen here, can have a devastating effect on life and limb

and it showed that the powder at both sites had a 17 per cent nitro-glycerine content as well as a stabilizing agent, nitro cellulose.

However, even this was considered not enough to convict, so detectives returned again to scour the bungalow at Fair Haven. This time they found a 9-volt battery used to detonate the bomb. On the underside was printed a sequence of letters and numbers which subsequently proved to be an identification code relating to a specific batch made on a particular day at a particular factory. Police later found an open packet of 9-volt batteries at Dean's house with the same batch numbers. One battery was missing.

And the final nail in Dean's coffin was the discovery of a file containing the fictitious return name and address in his computer. He had evidently deleted the file but wasn't aware that by printing the label he had created another file which could easily be recovered from the hard drive. Dean had assumed that no one would ever connect him with the bombing because he had never been to Fair Haven and had never met the victim. He was wrong and now has a lifetime in prison to regret it.

Truck driver and pipe bomber Christopher Dean at the time of his arrest

Lockerbie

Even the smallest fragment of evidence might prove to be the crucial clue that ultimately solves a case. The crash of Pan Am Flight 103 on 21 December 1988 is a prime example of how a major case can be solved by an apparently insignificant item.

A year after Pan Am Flight 103 had been blasted out of the sky over the remote Scottish town of Lockerbie investigators were no nearer to solving the case than they had been on day one. The tragedy had initiated one of the most exhaustive investigations of recent times with 200,000 fragments recovered from the debris of the town and the surrounding countryside. The only certainty was that an explosion had ripped through the plane's cargo bay and that it appeared to have been caused by a bomb as pieces of a triggering device had been found. But they were at a loss to say who might have been responsible.

It was by chance that a man out walking his dog happened to notice a small piece of grey fabric torn from a T-shirt near the crash site and brought it to the local police in the hope that it had a connection with the crash. The label was intact which led detectives to the owner of a small clothing shop in Malta. Incredibly the owner was able to give them a detailed description of the customer because the man had behaved oddly, buying several items without considering the style or size.

Chemical analysis revealed that the T-shirt had been used to wrap the bomb, but, more significantly, a shard from the circuit board bearing the number '1' was imbedded between the fibres which helped detectives to identify the timing device as a Swiss MST-13. When combined with other evidence, the fabric scrap and the fragment of circuit board led to the arrest of two Libyan agents working at Malta airport who had primed the bomb and sent it on to London using stolen luggage labels where it was loaded aboard the fateful flight.

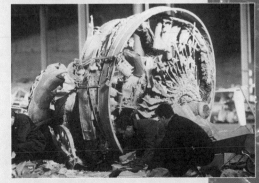

Investigators examine the remains of Pan Am Flight 103

case file

The King's Cross Fire

When 31 people died in a fire at King's Cross underground station in London on 18 November 1987, the authorities feared that it might have been the result of a terrorist bomb. The IRA were then active on the British mainland and the police needed to know as a matter of urgency if King's Cross was the first casualty in a new campaign of terror.

Although witnesses had reported seeing smoke billowing from beneath an escalator, suggestive of a small electrical fire, one of the victims had injuries that appeared to be consistent with those caused by an explosion. Fortunately, the pathologist in charge had considerable experience of both fire and terrorist attacks and was able to identify the wound to the young woman's leg as having been caused by molten debris. He ruled out a bomb but there was still the demanding task of identifying the cause of the blaze and reconstructing the sequence of events from clues to be found in the bodies. The nature of the injuries would tell the victim's stories now that they were no longer able to speak for themselves.

LESSONS TO BE LEARNED

It was critical to know if the deaths could have been avoided, not just for the sake of the bereaved families, but also for the future safety of the London Underground network. If there was a question of possible negligence the bereaved might be entitled to compensation or have grounds to sue those responsible. Health and safety officials would also have to learn from the disaster to ensure it could never occur again.

Forensically speaking, fires are not straightforward. Victims die in different ways, depending on where they are in relation to the flames and other factors. At King's Cross the pathologist's report revealed that some had died mercifully quickly in the vicinity of the fireball, which had generated heat around 1200° centigrade. However, it wasn't the heat that had killed them but the inhalation of cyanide created by the burning paint and ceiling tiles. Others were overcome by smoke, but many had simply been incinerated in the flashover and were found in the characteristic pugilist pose indicative of asphyxiation.

It emerged that the cause of the fire was a discarded cigarette or match which had dropped between the escalator treads and set alight oily rags or paper that had been allowed to accumulate under the escalator. The cause of the ensuing fireball remains a mystery, but the fire was certainly spread uncommonly rapidly by the huge draughts of air caused by the movement of the trains through the tunnels and by the anti-graffiti paint which acted as an accelerant.

But that wasn't the end of the matter. The pathologist's findings proved crucial in the case of fireman Colin Townsley, who had died trying to save passengers and been posthumously awarded the Queen's Gallantry Medal for Brave Conduct. Two years after his death his widow initiated a case for damages on the grounds that he had suffered 'pre-impact terror' which involves unnecessary suffering and asked for the forensic report to support her claim. The autopsy revealed that the fireman had not sustained severe burns but had died from the inhalation of fumes. He must have been conscious for several minutes and therefore aware of the fact that there was no hope of escape and that death was inevitable.

The cyanide vapour created by the burning paint and ceiling tiles had been such a deadly contributing factor that, in the aftermath of the disaster, flame-retardant paint became standard and a sprinkler system was installed. In addition all the old wooden escalators on the London Underground were ripped out and replaced by those made of metal. And as a further precaution smoking was banned throughout the underground system. Lessons had been learned, but at a terrible cost.

Underground damage: the top of the escalators at King's Cross after the fire

Policemen emerge from the charred remains of the tube station at King's Cross

Chapter 8
Suspect Science

There have been several high-profile miscarriages of justice in recent years, where an eagerness to secure a conviction has led to some questionable verdicts that have, on appeal, eventually been overturned and the defendants allowed to walk free. Forensic science is only as effective as the people who use it and, if they are blinded by ambition, professional pride or are simply incompetent, they can manipulate data and results as effectively and to the same destructive end as any criminal. Forensic techniques can be manipulated to create a false impression, as in cases of fraud and forgery but, in the right hands, science will ultimately reveal the truth.

CIVIL CASES

Forensic science is not solely used for solving crimes. It is also now routinely employed in civil actions when there is a question of negligence which, if proven, can result in awards totalling millions of pounds in compensation. Such cases would include claims for accidental injury against employers or local authorities as well as against private companies who may be responsible for the illegal dumping of toxic waste into public drinking water or onto sites designated for development.

A culture of litigation has always existed in the US, but since the 1990s there has been an unprecedented growth in civil actions across

Yves Montand whose body was exhumed to determine a paternity lawsuit after his death

Europe and as a result numerous private laboratories have been established offering expertise to parties who feel that they failed to secure justice through the criminal justice system and are now forced to pursue cases for compensation through the civil courts. In the US, the O. J. Simpson case is one notable example (see page 46). But the motive is not always financial nor even the pursuit of justice.

Several high-profile paternity suits have recently been determined using the same DNA analysis techniques that were originally developed to secure criminal convictions. In several cases the subject of the action was deceased when the test was carried out. The French actor Yves Montand, for example, was disinterred in 1998, seven years after his death, to allow DNA to be extracted so that a potentially costly lawsuit could be avoided and the matter of paternity resolved. DNA analysis was also recently employed to prove or disprove rumours that America's founding father and third president Thomas Jefferson had fathered an illegitimate child with his young black slave and companion Sally Hemings. DNA proved the truth of the allegation and a small but significant footnote will need to be added to all future biographies of the great man. A similar mystery surrounds George Washington, the first US President, who is thought to have fathered a child with a black slave living on his brother's estate. But while the girl's descendants are willing to donate DNA to settle the matter, the FBI

have failed to recover sufficient genetic material from locks of Washington's hair to carry out the test.

MISCARRIAGES OF JUSTICE

Both fictional and factual TV crime series give the false impression that forensic science is infallible and for that reason miscarriages of justice are now a thing of the past. But that is simply not true. Science is only as good as the scientists who use it, and sadly there are many recorded cases of pathologists, medical examiners and laboratory

Professor Meadows whose expert evidence was discredited – see p193

Justice at last: the release of the Birmingham Six in 1991

technicians who have repeatedly failed to interpret and present the evidence in the correct way, through negligence, arrogance or, in rare cases, even wilful falsification of their findings to enhance their own reputation.

In 2005 several women who had been wrongly imprisoned for murdering their own children in the so-called 'shaken baby syndrome' cases had their convictions quashed by the British Court of Appeal because the testimony of forensic paediatrician Professor Sir Roy Meadows was considered unreliable.

In 1991 the Birmingham Six, who had been falsely imprisoned for the IRA pub bombings of mainland Britain in 1974, were finally freed after spending almost 20 years in prison when it was accepted that the method of testing for explosive residue at the time of their trial was flawed. It transpired that the technique used for detecting nitroglycerine, known as the Griess test, would also register positive for other common substances such as nitro-cellulose which is a chemical used in the manufacture of playing cards and cigarette packets. Several of the suspects had been smoking and playing cards just prior to their arrest.

Confessions were allegedly beaten out of them, but at an earlier appeal hearing the judges are said to have deliberately ignored both accusations of police wrongdoing and the results of a later, far more reliable chemical test because they could not admit to the possibility that the British judicial system was not perfect.

These are only a handful of high-profile cases that made the headlines. To list all the modern miscarriages of justice that hinged solely on flawed forensic evidence would take a book all of its own.

A QUESTION OF INTERPRETATION

Such cases raise the question as to how far forensic scientists should go in interpreting their findings as fact and at what point interpretation of the facts becomes speculation. The facts should speak for themselves, but often the expert witness is asked to present a theory as the truth, the whole truth and nothing but the truth.

An extreme example is that of the Texas forensic psychiatrists who are asked to predict a defendant's future behaviour based on their past actions and the crime of which they are accused so that the jury can decide whether to recommend the death penalty or life imprisonment. While it may be possible to predict a person's future criminal behaviour, that prediction is conditional on the quality of the expert witness.

In Dallas, Texas forensic psychiatrist Dr James Grigson acquired the nickname 'Dr Death' because his assessment was frequently the deciding factor in whether a convicted person should live or die. But in 1977 Grigson testified that defendant Randall Dale Adams, who had been found guilty of murder, possessed a 'sociopathic personality disorder' and that he would, without doubt, kill again.

In fact, Adams was subsequently found to have been innocent of the crime of which he had been accused and had never killed anyone. Dr Grigson had evidently used his experience to speculate on the state of mind and future behaviour of the person who had committed the murder and not the person sitting opposite him in the courtroom on trial for his life. Mr Adams was released just three days before his scheduled execution.

UNTRUSTWORTHY SCIENTISTS

Unfortunately, in the state of Texas many men and women whose convictions are likely to be judged unsafe over the next few years will not walk free for the simple reason that they have been executed on the questionable findings of pathologist Ralph Erdmann and forensic serologist Fred Zain, who together are thought to account for several thousand wrongful convictions.

The cases of Erdmann and Zain are unrelated, but it is surely no coincidence that both occurred in the Lone Star State where there is abnormal pressure on forensic scientists to serve the interests of one party or the other in a prosecution because the ever-present spectre of the death penalty raises the stakes to a degree where there is absolutely no margin for error.

Zain only came to the attention of diligent public defender George Castelle because his record was simply too good to be true.

Between 1977 and 1993 Zain was called to testify at hundreds of rape and murder trials because he produced the results prosecutors needed to secure a conviction, often identifying blood and semen stains previous examinations had failed to find. The greater his reputation grew, the more cases he was given and these included many in neighbouring states. It was only in 1992 after a wrongly convicted man, Glen Woodall, successfully sued the state of West Virginia for wrongful imprisonment that Zain's ineptitude came to light.

Woodall had served five years for a rape he did not commit because Zain had testified that the semen recovered from the victim proved that the assailant's blood type was the same as Woodall's. While it may have been the same type, that does not necessarily mean that it was Woodall's blood.

The extent to which Zain's shoddy science impacted upon innocent people's lives was highlighted in a subsequent investigation, that of the black athlete William Harris.

The Harris case is a particularly disturbing example of how a misplaced faith in the infallibility of forensic science can sidetrack the justice system and cloud the judgment of those involved in the investigation. In 1985 Harris, a talented high-school student with a promising future in athletics, was accused of rape despite the fact that the victim had categorically ruled him out as her attacker from a photo line-up.

Harris had only been included in the line-up because he fitted the general description as being 'young, black and athletic'. This significant detail was not presented at trial and in fact the witness subsequently identified Harris as her attacker in court, having apparently been persuaded by the flawed forensic evidence that she must have been mistaken in initially ruling him out. Harris spent seven years in prison until DNA evidence finally proved his innocence.

At the conclusion of its investigation into Zain's career the West Virginia Supreme Court declared that Zain's 'systematic' errors involved 'overstating the strength of results ... reporting inconclusive results as conclusive,' and 'repeatedly altering laboratory records'.

But incredibly this catalogue of ineptitude was not an isolated incident. During the 1980s, while Zain was building an undeserved reputation for getting results, a colleague in the same state was abusing the trust placed in him with equally disastrous results. Forensic pathologist Dr Ralph Erdmann was fabricating autopsy reports, mislaying body parts and falsifying evidence which resulted in many murder victims being certified as having died from natural causes and their killers escaping capture. He was not only lazy and incompetent, he was also revealed to be over-eager in the extreme to please his employers and to produce the results they wanted.

Dr Erdmann's systematic abuse of his privileged position was only discovered when a bereaved family questioned his autopsy report which stated that he had removed and weighed the spleen of their loved one, a procedure that would have been impossible in this particular case as the deceased had had their spleen surgically removed many years before. As the prosecutor observed at the end of the investigation into Dr Erdmann's iniquitous career, 'If the prosecution theory was that death was caused by a Martian death ray, then that was what Dr Erdmann reported.'

But it wasn't the deceit or wilful negligence which had brought about his downfall. That had only led to the revoking of his medical licence and a demand for the repayment of his autopsy fees. Dr Erdmann was only put behind bars in the late 1990s when police found an M-16 assault rifle and a small armoury of other weapons at his home which violated the provisions of his probation.

A scientist places test tubes in the centrifuge for analysis

case file

The Hitler Diaries

When German investigative journalist Gerd Heidemann was offered a cache of Adolf Hitler's unpublished personal diaries, written in the Führer's own hand, he couldn't believe his luck. The Nazi leader's personal papers were believed to have been destroyed in April 1945 when the plane carrying them out of besieged Berlin was shot down over Dresden. No one had expected them to resurface.

So eager was Heidemann to secure the scoop of the century that he committed the cardinal sin of journalism – he failed to question the legitimacy of his source. Had he done so he would have discovered that the man he was so keen to do business with was a convicted forger.

Konrad Kajau had begun his criminal career forging luncheon vouchers, but quickly progressed to paintings before finally graduating to manufacturing Nazi memorabilia, for which there was a lucrative worldwide market.

Posing as a wealthy collector, Kajau conned Heidemann into believing that he was acting as an agent for an East German army officer who could not be named for fear of being sent to Siberia by his Russian superiors for smuggling a national relic to the West. Heidemann and his boss at Gruner and Jahr, one of Germany's leading magazine publishers, would have to take it on trust that the diaries were genuine and make a bid, or risk the offer being withdrawn.

So, on 18 February 1981, Heidemann attended a secret meeting with publishing director Manfred Fischer at which Fischer and his fellow executives approved the purchase of 27 diaries and several other manuscripts comprising the unpublished third volume of Hitler's autobiography, *Mein Kampf*, for the equivalent of $2million.

It was only after the delivery of the manuscripts that the triumphant journalist and his bosses thought it prudent to have them properly authenticated, but even at this crucial stage they made another fateful mistake. They handed over the diaries to two forensic experts who were, to say the least, not the ideal choice. Ordway Hilton was an American documents expert who was unfamiliar with Germanic script and Swiss forensic scientist Max Frei-Sulzer was a microbiologist. Crucially, neither was aware that some of the samples of Hitler's handwriting that they had been given to compare were themselves forgeries, created by the very same hand, that of Kajau.

DOUBTS SET IN

Once Gruner and Jahr convinced themselves they had established the authenticity of their latest asset, they began probing abroad for publishing partners, initiating a bidding war between Rupert Murdoch's global media empire and American giant *Newsweek*. Naturally both parties wanted to be certain they were buying the genuine article and so brought in their own experts. Murdoch sent noted historian Hugh Trevor-Roper to Switzerland to examine the documents, knowing the English academic's name would carry weight with scholars and the foreign press, but Trevor-Roper later claimed he felt overwhelmed by the sheer volume of material and also pressured by both parties to overlook glaring historical discrepancies which originated in a book published in 1962. He overcame his doubts and declared himself satisfied the documents were genuine.

But even while Trevor-Roper wrestled with his reservations German forensic experts were subjecting samples to stringent chemical analysis. Their findings were conclusive and damning. A simple ultraviolet test revealed that both the paper and bindings had been bleached with a chemical called blankophor which was not in use until the 1950s, while the official Nazi seals contained traces of viscose and polyester, both of which did not exist during the Second World War. Even the ink was modern and, when subjected to a chloride evaporation test, revealed that the diary entries had been written just a year before.

The fraud was exposed in open court where both Heidemann and Kajau received prison sentences of just under five years, Kajau being found guilty of forgery and Heidemann of misappropriating his employers' money.

Sentenced for forgery: Konrad Kajau

The Mummy in the Cupboard

It sounds like a scene from *Psycho*, but the case of the mummified corpse kept in a cupboard in a Welsh boarding house is one of the most bizarre true-crime cases on record. And the most extraordinary aspect is that the alleged murderer was not a psychopathic serial killer but the victim's middle-aged landlady, who lived with the grisly secret for 20 years before dissension among the experts prevented her conviction for murder.

The mummified remains were accidentally uncovered in April 1960, when the landlady's son broke into the locked cupboard on a landing to clear out what he believed were a former tenant's belongings. When his mother, Mrs Sarah Harvey, returned from a short stay in hospital she found the cupboard bare and police officers waiting to interview her. At first Mrs Harvey struck the police as a harmless old lady as she told them her lodger, Mrs Frances Knight, had moved out in April 1945 about the same time that a couple had asked her to store some of their personal belongings, then left taking the cupboard key with them.

The ailing, enfeebled figure elicited the sympathy of detectives who dutifully followed up the false leads she had given them, but when neither Mrs Knight nor the fictitious couple could be traced, the police ordered an autopsy to determine the identity of the corpse. However, it wasn't as simple as they hoped. Although the body was in a remarkable state of preservation thanks to a constant stream of warm, dry air which had retarded decomposition, the pathologist was unable to confirm it was the body of Mrs Knight. Dental records were of no use as the victim had false teeth and these had disappeared along with a wedding ring which might have proved identity. All that could be said with certainty was that the body was that of a white female aged between 40 and 60, who had been 163cm (5ft 4in) tall, right-handed and walked with a limp. Moreover, she shared the same blood group as members of Mrs Knight's family.

AN ODD STORY

It was clearly the mummy of Mrs Knight, but without a positive identification it could not be stated as a fact in a court of law.

Fortunately, Mrs Harvey broke down under questioning and admitted that she had concealed the body in a state of panic. But what reason could she have had for fearing anyone would have queried her version of events if Mrs Knight had died of natural causes as she claimed?

Harvey alleged that Mrs Knight had collapsed in her room on the day she died. Unable to lift her onto the bed, Harvey left her lodger on the floor. Yet when had she returned to find her lodger had died, she had miraculously found the strength to drag the body into the hall and stuff it into the cupboard along with a mattress to soak up the seeping body fluids.

However, she couldn't explain the stocking that had been tied around the neck of the corpse with a knot so tight that it had left a groove around the throat and an impression on the thyroid cartilage.

It appeared that Mrs Knight had been strangled, yet at the trial various forensic specialists disagreed as to the manner of death, with one even suggesting that she might have hanged herself and another that there was no evidence that the stocking had been tight enough to act as a ligature. The impressions on the neck, he argued,

65-year-old grandmother Sarah Harvey was not all she seemed

might have been caused by swelling in the neck post-mortem. Yet even if Mrs Knight had taken her own life, there would have been no reason for Mrs Harvey to conceal her body and in so doing bring suspicion upon herself.

With dissension among the experts, the judge was forced to direct the jury to find Mrs Harvey not guilty of murder. In the end she was convicted of fraud and sentenced to 15 months for having deceived Mrs Knight's solicitors into believing that the old lady was still alive so that she could draw her £2 maintenance payments every week for almost 20 years.

case file

The Angel of Death

Dr Josef Mengele's insatiable appetite for cruelty exceeded that of the most cold-blooded mad doctors of pulp fiction. The murderous Nazi was known as the Angel of Death because of his sadistic experiments on the helpless inmates of Auschwitz concentration camp, where he was personally responsible for the murder of 400,000 people, many of them children.

Mengele's name and the enormity of his crimes was unknown to the Allies when they liberated the concentration camps in 1945, allowing the 'Angel' to slip unnoticed through the chaos of post-war Europe and seek asylum in South America. It was only after the dramatic arrest and abduction of one of his colleagues, Adolf Eichmann, the architect of the 'Final Solution' from Argentina in 1961 to stand trial for war crimes that the search for Mengele was intensified. But it would be another 24 years before one of the most notorious mass murderers of modern times was finally captured.

In 1985, impelled by a fresh American initiative to bring Mengele to justice, two German expatriates domiciled in Brazil offered to take investigators to what they claimed was the burial site of the world's most wanted war criminal.

Naturally, both the American and German authorities demanded that their forensic experts be allowed to examine the remains and determine the identity of the man who had been buried under the name of Wolfgang Gerhard. But there was an additional group with claims to a special interest in the outcome – associates of the celebrated Nazi-hunter Simon Wiesenthal, who had himself been brutalized in Auschwitz. Together the three parties assembled a distinguished team of experts who travelled to the remote Brazilian town of Embu on 6 June 1985.

There they exhumed the coffin and examined its contents which were evidently those of a white, right-handed elderly male between sixty and seventy years of age. These basic facts could be determined by the narrowness of the pelvis, the shape of the skull, the comparatively longer bones on the right side and the degree of wear of the teeth and specific bones. A more accurate estimate of the age of the skeleton was indicated by the multitude of microscopic canals in the femurs which carry the blood vessels. The amount and condition of these indicated a man in his late sixties which would correspond to Mengele's age. The length of key bones gave a reliable height for the corpse of 173.5cm (5ft 7½in), half a centimetre short of the height recorded in Mengele's SS file.

But his dental record proved to be of little use as it was hand-drawn and light on detail, although it indicated a pronounced gap at the front of the upper palate which resulted in a characteristic gap-tooth grin. An X-ray of the skull confirmed that Herr Gerhard had possessed the very same distinctive feature.

In the final stage of the examination the skull provided the conclusive evidence that even the conspiracy theorists could not question. Using a technique known as video superimposition, German forensic anthropologist Richard Helmer overlaid a photograph of the skull onto archive photographs of Dr Mengele to reveal 30 key features that were a positive match.

Nevertheless there were those who feared the Angel of Death had eluded them yet again.

Then in 1992 the advent of genetic fingerprinting made it possible to compare DNA from the remains in Embu with a sample taken from one of Mengele's living relatives. There could be no doubt. The bones in Brazil were those of Dr Mengele.

case file

Jack the Ripper

There can be no doubt that had Scotland Yard possessed the tools and techniques of forensic science at the end of the 19th century they would have been able to identify and apprehend the first serial killer of modern times – Jack the Ripper. As it was, the routine fingerprinting of criminals was still several years in the future, basic blood grouping remained to be discovered and the value of trace evidence had still to be fully appreciated by the Metropolitan Police and proven in an English court of law.

Forensic detection was in its infancy in 1888, when the Ripper stalked the gloomy streets of Whitechapel disembowelling prostitutes before disappearing into the thick London fog. But he left several clues behind. At the site of the first murder, in Buck's Row, where he slit the throat of Mary Ann Nichols, the official records state that no significant clues were found, yet it is inconceivable he did not leave footprints in the grime and mud which could have been photographed, or at least sketched, so they could be compared with shoes belonging to the prime suspects.

THE BODY COUNT RISES

A month later, on 8 September, the body of Annie Chapman was discovered in a back yard at Hanbury Street, Spitalfields, with an envelope by her head and her meagre personal belongings arranged neatly at her feet as if part of a crude funeral ritual. All of these items might have preserved the killer's fingerprints. A leather apron, of which much was made at the time, proved to belong to a resident of the tenement. But little was made of the fact that her cheap brass rings had been wrenched from her fingers, suggesting that the killer mistook them for gold – an error an educated man would not have made. If the police had only thought to search their suspects' lodgings, they might have quickly wrapped up the case.

The nature of the mutilations and depth of the wounds led pathologist Dr George Bagster Phillips to conclude that the killer had some degree of medical knowledge. The Ripper had taken between 15 minutes and an hour to perform his hideous surgery, which led the coroner to speculate he might have experience of the post-mortem room, another observation which could have helped the police to narrow their shortlist of suspects.

As the hunt for the Ripper intensified, the body of Elizabeth Stride was found in Dutfield Yard off Berner Street on the morning of 30 September and later that same day a second victim, Catharine Eddowes, was discovered in Mitre Square. In nearby Goulston Street the Ripper had discarded a piece of bloodied cloth torn from Eddowes' apron on which he had cleaned his knife. Chalked on the wall above it were the words, 'The Juwes are the men that will not be blamed for nothing'. Fearing this might incite an anti-Jewish riot, Metropolitan Police Commissioner Sir Charles Warren had it removed.

Had he delayed until a photograph could be taken, posterity would have been availed of perhaps the most significant and revealing clue of all, assuming of course that the writing was in the Ripper's own hand.

AN EYE-WITNESS DESCRIPTION

At the scene of the last and most hideous murder in Miller's Court, where he dissected the body of Mary Kelly in a frenzied travesty of an autopsy, there must have been a wealth of trace evidence, hair, fibre and fingerprints, as the murder took place inside the victim's lodgings.

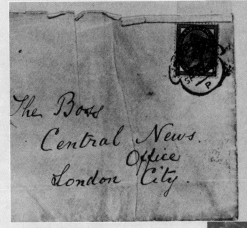

It is believed the killer may even have left behind a red handkerchief a witness had seen him give to Mary only an hour before, which a family member or friend might have recognized had the fact been publicized.

The detailed description which the eye witness gave of the man he saw soliciting Mary minutes before her death should have been sufficient to

Fragment of one of the most crucial overlooked clues in the history of crime

identify the Ripper, but even allowing for the fact that Scotland Yard had only recently formed its formidable Criminal Investigation Department (CID) they seemed curiously incapable of coordinating the eye-witness testimony and physical evidence so that they could at least eliminate some of their prime suspects. All of these crucial clues were overlooked or undervalued due to the laborious, unscientific method of crime detection which still prevailed in the UK at the time, and the stubborn belief that the way to catch a criminal was to apprehend him in the act.

POLICE LED ASTRAY

The police were further hampered by fictitious letters purporting to be from the Ripper which a modern forensic handwriting expert could have dismissed as bogus after a few hours' study. Instead they distracted detectives and drained much-needed resources. A third letter containing a note and part of a human kidney may well have been from the Ripper, but without a fully equipped forensic laboratory of the kind Edmond Locard was to establish in France in 1910, Scotland Yard was groping in the dark.

The other practical problem with which the police had to contend was the fact that sex killers were, and still are, notoriously difficult to catch because they are impulsive, erratic individuals who rarely conform to a predictable pattern of behaviour. It wasn't until the development of forensic profiling that a psychological sketch of the Ripper could be created based on his choice of victims, the nature of the mutilations and the location of the crime scenes.

In 1988, on the centenary of the Whitechapel murders, FBI agents Roy Hazelwood and John Douglas studied the documented evidence and concluded that the Ripper was probably a young white male whose volatile temperament and predisposition towards violent antisocial behaviour would have brought him to the attention of the police prior to the murders. He might therefore already have a conviction for affray or assault which would have been on file.

The fact that all the murders took place between midnight and 6am suggests that he lived alone, probably within 1.5–3km (1–2 miles) of the crime scenes as he knew the area well enough to escape undetected. Predatory killers usually begin stalking their prey in the vicinity of their own homes or place of business, moving further out as their confidence grows. In contrast to the slumming aristocrat depicted in popular fiction, he would have been of unkempt appearance and was likely to have been employed in mundane labour with little or no contact with the public, such as a slaughterman or dock worker.

And so the conclusion has to be that it was not the lack of physical evidence or eye-witness descriptions but the inability of the authorities to understand the significance of what they had and to act upon it that allowed Jack the Ripper to become the most enduring mystery in criminal history – the archetypal 'one that got away'.

The Finger of Suspicion

Dr Sam Sheppard and his wife Marilyn were the image of the all-American couple. Dr Sam, as he was known locally, was an even-tempered young man of considerable personal charm with a profitable practice as an osteopath in Bay Village and a large executive-style home in a leafy suburb of Cleveland which the couple shared with their six-year-old son Chip. But their seemingly idyllic world was shattered when, on the night of 3 July 1954, Mrs Sheppard was found brutally beaten to death in the first-floor bedroom and her husband was accused of her murder.

Dr Sheppard claimed to have been asleep on the living room couch when he heard Marilyn cry out. Bolting up the stairs he had entered the bedroom where he was confronted by a shadowy figure who struck him over the head. When he finally recovered his senses, he stated that he heard the intruder escaping out the back door and gave chase. There in the darkness he saw the silhouette of a bushy-haired man who wheeled around and struck a second disabling blow from which he did not recover until the police arrived.

From the moment the Coroner, Dr Samuel Gerber, was put on the case he began questioning Dr Sheppard's version of events. To Gerber's eyes the scene appeared to have been staged, with drawers pulled out of a bureau and neatly stacked on the floor, Dr Sheppard's surgical bag emptied and placed in the hallway where it would catch the investigator's eyes and a bag of valuables stashed in a bush at the bottom of the garden. Inside the bag police found the doctor's blood-splattered self-winding watch which had stopped at 4.15am. Fingerprints had also been hastily erased, supporting the possibility that a third person had been present, but it seemed highly unlikely that an intruder could have failed to notice Dr Sheppard sleeping in the lounge and left him unmolested while he attacked his wife.

The finger of suspicion began to point to Dr Sheppard, and as the investigation dug deeper it emerged that both Sam and Marilyn Sheppard had had affairs. The whiff of scandal brought the local media baying for the doctor's blood. While the inexperienced local investigators dragged their feet and tried to cover up the fact that they had contaminated the crime scene in their carelessness, the local press demanded that their prime suspect be arrested. Before the week was out the press were setting the agenda and the subsequent trial seemed to be a mere formality.

For reasons best known to himself, Dr Gerber let it be known that the murder weapon was a surgical instrument. And it was this more than any other single piece of evidence which sealed Sheppard's fate. It later transpired that the murder weapon had not been found and that the coroner had made his assumption based on a suspicious 'shape' impressed in the pillow next to the body.

One thing that might explain Dr Gerber's stubborn refusal to face the facts was that he considered Dr Sheppard to be a thorn in his side. There was said to be personal animosity and distrust between the two medical men. Dr Sheppard was known to disapprove of the coroner's approach to forensic investigation and so bruised pride may have been a factor in Gerber's overlooking, and perhaps even suppressing, significant clues. It is known, for example, that evidence of forced entry at the doors to the basement was never presented in court. Furthermore, there were blood spots on the basement steps which had presumably dripped from the weapon as there were no indications the assailant had been injured.

Dr Gerber presented these blood spots as evidence of Dr Sheppard's guilt. At that time there was no available method of determining whose blood had been found, only whether it was animal or human. But Dr Sam's performance on the witness stand gave his defence counsel cause for concern. He recollected the horrific events with an almost academic detachment. When questioned about the events leading to the discovery of his wife's battered body, he remarked, 'I initiated an attempt to gather enough senses to navigate the stairs.'

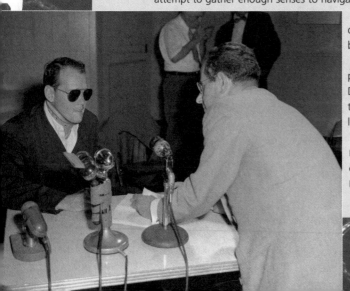

Hardly the kind of tone one would expect of a bereaved husband.

Dr Sam's poor performance, together with Dr Gerber's testimony, helped to secure a conviction and a life sentence. However, the

Dr Sam Sheppard (left) is questioned by his nemesis Dr Samuel Gerber

forensic evidence suggested that Sheppard might have been telling the truth. Although Marilyn had been repeatedly beaten until her face was unrecognizable the assailant had not used sufficient force to kill her. She had, in fact, drowned in her own blood. Dr Sheppard was a strong well-built man who could easily have killed someone with a single blow using a blunt weapon. Moreover, it is extremely unlikely that he would have bludgeoned his wife to death while their son slept in the next room, no matter how enraged he might have been. More revealing was the blood splatter on the wall and bedroom door to the left of the body which indicated spray from a weapon wielded by a left-handed assailant. Dr Sheppard was right-handed.

With such significant discrepancies a second trial was inevitable. At the retrial in 1964 the defence made much of Dr Gerber's failure to find the murder weapon, casting doubt on his assertion that it had been a surgical instrument. Greater attention was paid to the significance of the blood splatter and the 'flying blood' spray found on the inside of Dr Sheppard's watch strap, intimating that he had not been wearing it during the frenzied attack, but that it might have been in the possession of an intruder, as Sheppard had insisted.

It was suggested that the blood trail in the basement had been left by a casual labourer named Richard Eberling who had worked for the Sheppards and who was later incarcerated for killing several women. He was known to wear a wig to cover his thinning hair which might account for the bushy-haired figure Dr Sheppard claimed to have seen. Eberling even confessed, but his confession was dismissed due to his mental instability.

With more than sufficient reasonable doubt Dr Sheppard was acquitted the second time round, but ten years in prison had taken their toll. He left court a broken man, unfit to practise medicine, and died four years later.

However, his son continued to campaign to clear his father's name and in 1997 he filed a $2 million lawsuit against the state of Ohio supported by DNA evidence proving that the stains on the basement stairs were not his father's blood.

It appears that Eberling, a diagnosed schizophrenic, had become obsessed with Marilyn and must have killed her when she refused his advances. Dr Gerber, however, would not entertain the idea that he might have helped to convict the wrong man and there are those who even now still harbour doubts as to Dr Sam's innocence.

Index

A

abductive reasoning 42-3
Adams, Randall Dale 194
Addington, Anthony 16
ageing effect 152-3
Allard, M 28
'American method' 138
Anastasia 146-8
Anderson, Ellen 76
Anderson, Rosemary 175-7
Antistius 13
arson 123, 168-9
Ashworth, Dawn 108-9
audio isolation 91
audio restoration 91, 110
audio-visual, overview 90
autopsy 118-23, 180

B

Baker, Michelle 100-1
ballistic science 22, 88, 89, 164-5
Balthazard, Victor 165
Bell, Larry Gene 158-9
Bertillon, Louis-Adolphe 18, 59, 62
'Birmingham Six' 192-3
Blackburn, Estelle 176-7
Blandy, Mary 16
blood
    bloodstains 52-4
    DNA analysis 52
    phenolphthalein 36
    splatter science 52-4
    types 52
Bocarme, Count Hippolyte de 102-3
Boomerang 21
Brown, Debra 117
Button, John 175-7

C

Canter, David 161-2
case files
    abduction and murder 157-9
    Anderson hit and run death 175-7
    battered widow 76
    delivery man murder 97-9
    digital identikit 152-3
    drive-by shooting 33, 33, 70-1
    Hitler diaries 196-7
    Hughes, Howard, ghost writer 104-7
    iron age murder 143-5
    Kennedy, John F K 178-81
    King's Cross St Pancras station fire 186-8
    Le Havre investigation 23-5
    Libyan Embassy 121, 172-4
    Lockerbie bombing 167, 185
    MacIvor case 149-51
    Maxwell, Robert 127-34
    Miami mugging 154-6
    Mitchell brothers 170-1
    Mowbray widow 63-5
    mummified corpse 198-199
    nicotine poisoning 102-3
    paint scraping 92-3
    Pan Am flight 103: 185
    pipe bomb murder 33, 182-4
    poisoned by doctor 100-1
    Praslin affair 26-8
    railway rapist 160-2
    Russian royal family 146-8
    schoolgirls raped and murdered 108-9
    Simpson murder case 46-50, 191
    Stratton Brothers 60-2
    teenager murder 94-6
    Urschel kidnap 66-9
    Watergate 110
    wife killer 124-6
    woodchip killer 72-5
Castelle, George 194
cause of death 114-16
Chapman, Annie 202

Choiseul-Praslin, Duc de 26-8
CODIS, criminal database 9
Coleman, Alton 117
comparison polarized light microscope 82
Connally, Senator 179
Cooke, Eric Edgar 176-7
Cornet, Stanley 155-6
coroner 44-5
Crafts, Richard and Helle 72-5
crime laboratory, overview 78
crime scene
    bombs 166-8
    clues 33
    exterior location 32-3
    grid search 34
    initial impression 31-2
    interior location 31-2
    reconstruction software 90-1
    securing the scene 30-1
    terrorist act 33
crime-scene investigators (CSI)
    crime scene 35
    field kit 36-7
    forensic profile 39-40
criminal profiler 42
Cromarty, Hannah 61
CSI - Crime Scene Investigation 6-9
Culshaw, Edward 164-5
Cummings, Homer S 19-22, 69
cyanosis 44
cytotec 100-1

D

dactyloscopy 60
Dahme, Hubert 19-20
Dead Reckoning: The Art of Forensic Detection 42
Dean, Christopher 183-4
dissection 120-1
Djurovic, Vesna 131
DNA analysis
    basics 81
    bloodstains 52
    development 22
    genetic code 'fingerprinting' 45, 79-81, 108-9
    laboratory 78-80
    paternity cases 191
    polymerase chain reaction (PCR) 81, 82
    profiling 79-81
    restrictive fragment length polymorphisms (RFLP) 81
    short tandem repeats (STR) 80
Douglas, John 204
Drager tube 38
drowning 123, 132
Duffy, John 161-2

E

Eberling, Richard 207
Eddowes, Catharine 203
Edinburgh, HRH Duke of 148
Eichmann, Adolf 58, 200
Erdmann, Ralph 194, 195
Erwin, Tammy 100-1
ethnicity 135-6
eyes 116

F

facial reconstruction 138-40
Faulds, Henry 18, 62
Febvre, Laura Le 155-6
Felts, Lewis 70-1
fibres 84-5, 97-8
Fidelis, Fortunato 13
fingerprints
    analysis 39-40, 56
    development 18
    evaluation 58-9
    Great Train Robbery 56
    identification of victims 45
    key case 60-2
    kit 37, 38

vacuum metal deposition chamber 88
Fiorenza, Johnny 97-9
fire 123, 168-9
firearms 22, 88, 89, 164-5
Fletcher, Yvonne 172-4
footprints 54, 94
forensic anthropology 135-42
forensic artist 140-1
forensic evidence 131
forensic photography 40-2
forensic profile 142, 149-51, 152-3
forensic science history 12-22
forensic sculptors 138-40
Forfarazzo 29
Fougnies, Gustave 102-3
Frei-Sulzer, Max 196-7
Fuhrman, Mark 47-8
Fukada, Asaka 168

G

Garrison, Jim 181
Garson, Dr 62
Gerber, Dr Samuel 205-7
glass 86
Goddard, Henry 165
Goldman, Ronald 46-50
Great Train Robbery 56-7
Greenberg, Bernard 117
Griess test 193
Grigson, James 194
ground penetrating radar 36, 37
Grubbs, Julie 70-1
Gruner and Jahr 196-7

H

Haag, Lucian 171
Haight, W R 'Rusty' 176-7
hair 97-8
hanging 123
Harley, Leslie 76
Harris, William 194-5
Harvey, Sarah Jane 198-9
Hazelwood, Roy 204
Heidemann, Gerd 196-7
Heinrich, Dr Edward O 111-2
Helnick, Debra May 158
Hemings, Sally 191
Hendricks, David and Susan 124-6
Herschel, J F William 18, 20
Hewitt, Deborah A 39-40
Hillery, Booker T jnr 94-6
Hilton, Ordway 196-7
Hinman, Dayle 149-51
histology 122
Hitler diaries 196-7
Hoadley, R Bruce 75
Hollien, Harry 171
Hoover, J Edgar 69
Hughes, Helga R 106
Hughes, Howard 104-7
Humes, Commander 180

I

infrared micro spectrophotometer 82
injection, fatal 122
innocent men condemned to death 16
insect infestation 116-17
Irving, Clifford 104-7
Israel, Harold 19-22

J

Jack the Ripper 162, 202-4
Jefferson, Thomas 191
Jeffreys, Alec 79, 108-9

K

Kajau, Konrad 196-7
Kelly, 'Machine Gun' 66-9
Kelly, Ian 109
Kelly, Mary 203
Kennedy, John F K 178-81
Kersta, Lawrence 106
King's Cross St Pancras station

fire 186-8
Knight, Frances 198-9
Kowaleski, Joe 33, 70-1

L

Ladefoged, Peter 106
Lady Ghislaine 128, 130, 131-4
laser trajectory kit 37
Lathon, Ty 33, 70-1
Lee, Henry C 72-5
Letelier, Orlando 141
Levine, Lowell 147
Libyan Embassy 121, 172-4
ligor mortis 116
Lindow Man 143-5
List, John 152-3
Locard's exchange principle 118
Locard, Edmond 204
Lockerbie bombing 167, 185
Lovernios 144
Luest, Helga 154-6
Lyons, John 97-9

M

MacDonell, Herbert Leon 54, 63-4, 76
MacIvor, Michael and Missy 149-51
Macnaghten, Melville 60-2
'magic bullet' 179
Mann, Lynda 108-9
Maples, William 146
Marquis, Chris 33, 182-4
Maxwell, Christine 127-8
Maxwell, Robert 120, 127-34
Mayo, Keith 72, 75
Mazel, Lady 13-14
McFadden, Vincent 161-2
Meadows, Sir Roy 192-3
Mengele, Dr Josef 200-1
microscope 26, 28, 82-3
Miller, Marilyn 94-6
miscarriages of justice
    Adams, Randall Dale 194
    'Birmingham Six' 192-3
    Button, John 175-7
    Harris, William 194-5
    interpretation of evidence 193-4
    Maltese man executed 16
    Mowbray, Susie 63-5
    'shaken baby syndrome' 193
    Woodall, Glen 194
Mitchell, Artie and James 170-1
Montand, Yves 190, 191
Morgagni 13
morphometrics 138-40
Mowbray, Bill and Susie 63-5
Muir, Richard 62
Muntzing, Maynard 100-1
Mysteries of Police and Crime 16

N

Nichols, Mary Ann 202
Nixon, Richard 110-12
Nordby, Jon J 42

O

Oklahoma City bombers 167
Orfila 15-16
Oswald, Lee Harvey 178-9
Overton, Thomas 150-1

P

paint 83, 92-3, 96
Pan Am flight 103: 185
pedestrian crash reconstruction 176-7
'Pete Marsh' 143-5
Peters, Dr 180
Phillips, George Bagster 203
pipe bomb murder 33, 182-4
Pitchfork, Colin 109
poison
    arsenic 14-16, 28
    cytotec 100-1

nicotine 102-3
overview 87
strychnine 118
vegetable 103
police errors
    Button, John 175-7
    Jack the Ripper 202-4
    Simpson investigation 46-50
primer gunshot residue (P-GSR) 164
psychological profile 161-2
Purkinje, Johannes 59

R

Reiss, R A 23-5
Reynolds, Bruce Richard 57
Richardson 18
rigor mortis 114, 116, 132-3
Romero, Virgilio Paz 141
'Russian method' 140
Ryabov, Gely 146

S

Santos, Laura E 44-5
Schanzkowska, Franzisca 148
Schwartz, Charles 111-2
semtex 167, 168
serology tests 52
sexual assault kit 37
'shaken baby syndrome' 193
Sheppard, Dr Sam 205-7
Sheppard, Marilyn 205-7
Simpson, Nicole Brown 46-50
Simpson, O J 46-50, 191
Sims, Bernard 131
skeletal development 137
Smith, Shari Faye 157-9
Souviron, Richard 155-6
spalling 168-9
Stas, Jean Servais 102-3
stomach contents 116
Stratton, Albert and Alfred 60-2
Stride, Elizabeth 203

T

Tardieu, Ambroise 28
tattoos 122-3
Taylor, Karen T 141
thermal imager 37-8
time of death 114, 116, 124-6, 131-2
Titterton, Nancy 97-9
torture 16, 17
Townsley, Colin 187
toxicology 87
trace evidence 82-3, 96, 118
Tracey, Bernard 152-3
Treatise on Poisons 16
tree expertise 75
Trevor-Roper, Hugh 197
tyre and footprint casting kit 37
tyre tracks 54-6, 94

U

Urschel, Charles 66-9

V

Vannatrer, Philip 48
video enhancement 90
voice activated recording 110-12
voice disguise 158
voiceprint analysis 106

W

Walter, Richard 152-3
Warren, Sir Charles 203
Washington, George 191
West, Iain 131-4, 172-4
Wheat, Vernita 117
Woodall, Glen 194
Woods light 119
wound anlaysis 121-2

Z

Zacchia, Paolo 13
Zain, Fred 194-5
Zapruder, Abraham 178